T0290101

PRIDE
BEFORE
THE
FALL

Ryan Conway

PRIDE BEFORE THE FALL

How Derby County
went from Play-Off Final
to Near Extinction

First published by Pitch Publishing, 2023
Reprinted, 2023
2

Pitch Publishing
9 Donnington Park,
85 Birdham Road,
Chichester,
West Sussex,
PO20 7AJ
www.pitchpublishing.co.uk
info@pitchpublishing.co.uk

© 2023, Ryan Conway

Every effort has been made to trace the copyright.
Any oversight will be rectified in future editions at the
earliest opportunity by the publisher.

All rights reserved. No part of this book may be reproduced,
sold or utilised in any form or transmitted in any form or by
any means, electronic or mechanical, including photocopying,
recording or by any information storage and retrieval system,
without prior permission in writing from the Publisher.

A CIP catalogue record is available for this book
from the British Library.

ISBN 978 1 80150 503 1

Typesetting and origination by Pitch Publishing
Printed and bound in Great Britain by TJ Books, Padstow

Contents

Contents

Introduction

IT IS a privilege to cover Derby County and it was my ultimate honour to report on them during my two years as a full-time journalist. Fresh off the back of a heartbreaking Championship play-off final loss while things changed with the outgoings of fresh, young and exciting talent – the arrow was still seemingly pointing upwards with equally fresh and exciting imports.

To cover Derby from the summer of 2019 until the summer of 2021 saw the club go from one extreme to the other, and being able to keep on top of everything from on-field matters to takeovers to EFL charges, appeals and counter-appeals was a lot. But it was also a complete thrill and I look back on it with fondness, which is permitted now the club is in a fine and stable place, thankfully.

The lows of the play-off final defeat were followed by the highs of Phillip Cocu and Wayne Rooney arriving, followed by the lows of EFL charges, points deductions, a relegation battle and then, perhaps inevitably considering the circumstances, relegation itself. But they were all followed by the highest of highs which was David Clowes's takeover of the club. To say it has been an emotional four years between losing at Wembley to Aston Villa and the summer of 2023 when this book was finished would be an understatement. But throughout all the trials and tribulations Derby fans have stayed loyal in their support, they have made themselves heard when they felt invisible and not listened to, and they have shown what can happen when thousands of people have a common goal and pull together to make that happen. Even amid the unpleasantness of it all, it was a privilege to cover a club with such a dedicated fanbase.

Derby County fans deserve to know what is happening at their club, and what has happened at their club over what has been one of the most brutal periods of their history. When this book was first conceived it was to be a document of everything that had gone on. So many reports had been written in so many different places, and so many different people had so many different accounts of things – it felt right to put it all in one place so supporters, new and old, can look back on this period between these pages.

During my time covering the club I tried to do so with the utmost integrity, determination, passion and transparency. That does not mean I always got things right. Just simply that I tried to get things right – and not for me, for all of you. I saw myself as a conduit between club and fan, a spokesperson for frustrated supporters who did not have a platform as big as mine to speak out on some of the awful goings-on. I hope, in some way, I achieved that. Thank you for allowing me to cover our wonderful club.

Finally, I'd like to say thank you to my wonderful wife Anea. Without you this project would have never seen the light of day. Thank you for all your belief in me, thank you for all the encouragement, love and support. I love you.

Acknowledgements

I EXTEND my thanks to Curtis Davies, Max Lowe and Duane Holmes for their time in being interviewed for this book.

The following people were approached regarding this project but declined to comment: Wayne Rooney, Liam Rosenior, Martyn Waghorn, David Clowes, Paul Warne, Phillip Cocu.

The following were also approached but did not respond to requests for comment: Shay Given, Ravel Morrison, Chris Kirchner, Kornell McDonald, Jayden Bogle, Chris Martin, Quantuma, Erik Alonso.

Glasgow Rangers were approached with a view to speaking to Tom Lawrence, but the club did not respond to request for comment.

Mel Morris initially responded to a request for comment, before not responding to further communication.

The following publications were referenced:

The Athletic UK, BBC Radio Derby, BBC, Sky Sports, *Derby Telegraph, Daily Telegraph, Daily Mail, Daily Mirror, Mail on Sunday, The Sun, The Times, The Guardian, The Beautiful Game Podcast, JuddyTalks* podcast, RamsTV, Derby County website, NewsAtDen, Transfermarkt, *Rampage Magazine*, EFL.

Prologue

DERBY COUNTY have witnessed both ends of the extreme spectrum of sport. The dizzying highs of Wembley, thrilling all-guns-blazing football under Steve McClaren and Frank Lampard, and the heartbreak of Wembley, the play-off final losses, the brutal cruelties of the game that bring tears of sorrow rather than joy. Most of all, the club has confronted the depressing lows of administration threatening its very existence – all of this of course in the Mel Morris era.

The now former owner is often described by those who know him as thoughtful and kind, but also a bit of a loose cannon at times, perhaps somebody who could say one thing and then do the other – and always brash. As of the summer of 2023 Morris has retreated to a quieter life. There has been no big back-page interview from him (yet), no more fallout from Steve Gibson and Rob Couhig – the owners of Middlesbrough and Wycombe Wanderers respectively, who took particular umbrage with how Morris had circumnavigated EFL rules prior to their clubs missing out on the play-offs and being relegated at the expense of the Rams.

Between all of that has been a menagerie of incidents, from drink-driving accidents to late wage payments, phantom takeovers and, of course, the signing of Wayne Rooney. Not to mention the lengthy battles with the English Football League. Fans were being pulled from pillar to post, as were many of the staff at the club. Between 2019 and 2022 it had never been a more stressful time to be a Derby County supporter, member of staff, coach, manager, player, owner or journalist – bless the club's communications and media department for having to field 100 phone calls a day on this and that, giving the corner flag image a real workout for over three years on various statements. One can smile now, maybe even laugh – if you're sick enough. But that's only because everything is all right finally.

A fightback is being led by new owner David Clowes. The property expert, who swooped in to purchase Derby when the club was just days away from going bust amid 'the worst administration' some experienced football people had ever seen, has made an extraordinary impact both on and off the pitch without really saying a word. His withdrawn, humble approach is the antithesis of everything Morris was as a Derby owner, and it's a welcome change for many.

But the journey from Morris to Clowes has been an arduous one. It was never meant to be this way really. There was a brief period when fans had hopes that Derby would be one of the richest clubs in the world when a proposed takeover from BZI was 'imminent' – a word everybody got used to from 2020. The deal had its complications; credible journalists were reporting it was both still on and being called off as the game of public brinkmanship and trying to control the message spilled out across Twitter timelines and column inches everywhere. In the end, the deal did indeed collapse. No matter – Spanish businessman Erik Alonso had plans of bringing in players from all over Europe and had highlighted some of football's best and brightest to lead Derby to the Champions League in a decade. The deal collapsed. Never mind; Chris Kirchner, who many may say was a younger, American version of Morris – with a Twitter account – was coming in to save the club. He also had huge plans. His phantom takeover was the most sophisticated, as Kirchner even decked himself out in Derby gear, would interact with Derby fans, and would announce he would actually be the actual next owner. He made supporters really believe that their club was saved. His takeover failed. Twice. And he has been suspended from his own company, from which many of his staff had not been paid for months. Then the FBI raided his house in February 2023.

So now here we are. But to understand where Derby County are right now – one must go back to where they have come from.

In 2019 Derby were on the brink of returning to English football's top tier after an 11-year absence. In retrospect, it is a sliding-doors moment. Their 2-1 defeat to Aston Villa in the Championship play-off final is an even more bitter pill to swallow now with what has happened to both clubs in the meantime since that sun-kissed May afternoon.

For most of the 2018/19 season, former Chelsea legend Frank Lampard was dazzling during his rookie season as manager, employing free-flowing football with Mason Mount, Harry Wilson, Martyn Waghorn and Jack Marriott all reaching double figures for goals. The team scored three goals or more on eight occasions.

They knocked out Manchester United in the League Cup on penalties, before narrowly losing 3-2 to Chelsea, and suffered a similarly close 2-1 defeat to Brighton & Hove Albion in the fifth round of the FA Cup.

Then there was the famous night at Elland Road – one that has perhaps built Lampard's reputation as a whole, which has cemented Jack Marriott as cult hero. Having lost the first leg of the play-off semi-final 1-0 at Pride Park, and being largely outplayed in defeat – Derby didn't muster a single shot on target at their home ground – the signs were ominous for the trip to Yorkshire. Derby had lost all three games against Leeds United up to this point across the season, including a 2-0 defeat when they last visited Elland Road in January 2019.

Further strife then struck when Duane Holmes, who was in the starting XI, suffered a thigh tear during the warm-ups. The American midfielder pushed through the pain barrier and managed 44 minutes before being withdrawn for Marriott. But at that stage Derby were already 1-0 down on the night and 2-0 on aggregate. But in a sudden moment things changed.

Mason Bennett flicked on a long ball which Marriott chased down, applying pressure to centre-back Liam Cooper, who got into an awful mix-up with goalkeeper Kiko Casilla, allowing Marriott a simple finish and Derby a way back into the game right on the stroke of half-time. Loan stars Mount and Wilson gave Derby a surprising 3-2 lead heading into the final half an hour, before Stuart Dallas, who opened the scoring on the night, netted again to make it 3-3 just after the 60-minute mark.

With tensions on the pitch and in the stands reaching a nail-biting climax, Marriott struck again. Richard Keogh, who inexplicably found himself some 30 yards inside the Leeds half on a gut-busting run, slipped in a delightful one-touch through ball to Marriott, who dinked it over Casilla.

Bedlam ensued on the touchline, on the pitch and in the stands. Derby managed to hold on to make their way to Wembley and condemn one of their fiercest rivals to one of their most painful defeats.

The game itself was an ill-tempered affair with nine yellow cards and two reds as the backdrop to the occasion made for undoubted drama following Spygate, Leeds chants aimed at Frank Lampard crying, Leeds thoroughly outplaying the Rams for the prior three matches and the general spikiness and dislike for each other.

Victory at Wembley would have capped off the most magical of seasons, with an influx of young talent and a young manager at the helm trying to shed his playing skin. But it wasn't to be. Some of Lampard's decision-making for the final raised question marks – specifically the decision to once again place Marriott on the bench, despite his heroics.

Marriott was not prolific during his first season with Derby. A record of 13 goals in 43 appearances in all competitions (one every three games) was decent, but perhaps more was expected from the man the Rams paid £3m for that summer. What he was, however, was clutch.

Marriott netted winners against Sheffield United, Sheffield Wednesday and the dramatic finish in the thrilling 4-3 victory over Norwich City, all before his two-goal superhero act at Elland Road. In the final, with just under half an hour to play and 2-0 down once more, Marriott was summoned from the bench. He scored again. With nine minutes left to play. And this time it was not enough. The final whistle not only signalled the end of Derby's Premier League hopes for at least another season – it signalled the end of Lampard's brief stint at the club.

Chelsea and their Italian manager, Maurizio Sarri, had come to an agreement to let their latest incumbent return to his homeland and lead Juventus. The relationship was never that close and despite winning the Europa League, Sarri was unloved in London. When it came to finding a successor, Roman Abramovich went somewhat against his usual *modus operandi* and set about bringing Lampard back to the club as their new, and still relatively untested, head coach.

It was another hammer blow to Derby – not only losing out on a place in the Premier League, not only seeing the sparkling loan signings leave them, but now losing their manager. The £4m received in compensation was helpful, but hardly lessened the sting at the time. Though in hindsight, it is now easy to see why Morris drove such a hard bargain, if he read the tea leaves and knew Derby were going to need a lot of finances from somewhere.

Lampard had created a bond with the fans due to his outgoing nature and the excitable team he had created – brimming with youth and fearlessness, and naivety at times. Still rather fresh out of retirement, he walked the line of 'being one of the boys' and being a manager – and while it had its merits, there were also growing pains to come with it. After losses, Lampard could be down and dejected, at times rather thin-skinned to lines of questioning.

Even with Lampard's departure and the returning of loan superstars Mason Mount, Fikayo Tomori and Harry Wilson to their parent clubs (Chelsea for the former two, Liverpool for Wilson), to the outside world a bright future beckoned.

But Derby's squad still represented a decent core. After all, in the summer of 2018 they had spent heavily in recruiting Marriott (reported to be £3m), Martyn Waghorn (speculated to be around £5m), Florian Jozefzoon (£2.75m according to reports), Duane Holmes (believed to have been around £250,000), George Evans (for approximately £1m) and Scott Malone (for an unknown fee). Add to that the crop of academy prospects starting to push for first-team places – including Max Bird, Jason Knight, Jayden Bogle, Lee Buchanan, Max Lowe and Louie Sibley – and there was a reason to believe Derby's next superstars would come from within.

To add to that, three-time Eredivisie-winning manager Phillip Cocu walked through the door as Lampard's replacement, shortly followed by Manchester United and England's all-time record goalscorer Wayne Rooney – though he would not officially join until January 2020.

That hope soon turned sour; Cocu went from a decent top-half finish to being sacked after just 11 games the following season when Derby were bottom of the Championship. A litany of EFL charges, claims, counter-claims, appeals and counter-appeals would follow. The potential points deductions varied from three to 21, the latter of which the club ultimately received, and a desperate final-day battle to stay up was followed up with a season swimming against the tide and, due to the 21-point deduction, ultimately relegation to the third tier of English football for the first time since last going down in 1984.

Mel Morris's reign as owner of his boyhood club came to a brutal and unedifying end. His tenure could be summarised by reckless spending, near misses and, ultimately, taking Derby County backwards from their intended destination and almost putting the club out of existence. Though he still has his supporters, his reputation within the fanbase has dribbled away. And although many believe his heart was always in the right place when it came to what he wished for Derby to achieve, the strategy was not; 'There was never any strategy,' one source close to Morris said. Pinballing from high-priced transfers to a heavy youth movement, from swashbuckling football to pragmatic, to tried and tested managers to complete novices – the more Morris clutched at straws, the shorter they became.

Derby do have hope again, but a very different kind of hope. Dreams of being a Premier League club once more are perhaps further away than ever before – but at least they still exist, which is a victory in itself. Fans can still turn up to Pride Park and watch Derby County do what they do best – play football. The turnout is less about the anxiety of whether the next game will be the final one in the club's history, but a rallying cry to get the Rams back to where everybody feels they belong. A founding member of the Football League has now begun its slow climb back. Not even back to the top, just back to being a club that its fans and local community recognise. Much of the damage has indeed been repaired under Clowes and new manager Paul Warne, who took over from Liam Rosenior a quarter of the way into the 2022/23 season. But there is still a way to go, and, as I write, Derby still have some choppy waters to navigate – most obviously in the squad, with many of the players on short-term deals. But, finally, they are under no pressure to sell their best and brightest. Max Bird and Eiran Cashin won't be moving without a fight – and a hefty price tag – which means everybody can finally sleep a little easier at night. It's been a long road to freedom.

1

A Silver Lining and New Beginnings

EVEN IN the smouldering ashes of defeat, spirits were still high. After the 2-1 play-off final heartbreak against Aston Villa at Wembley, owner Mel Morris insisted the players and staff go back to Pride Park to celebrate what had been a successful season all told. Although the club had fallen short of their ultimate goal of Premier League football, now was not the time to dwell. The influx of youthful talent blended together by a young management team and coaching staff was something to be celebrated. Perhaps more so because Morris knew how short-lived the experience would be and he would soon have to go about the task of putting together a new coaching staff and investing once again in the squad. It was made clear early on that the funds would be a lot tighter than under Frank Lampard, though Morris did still find enough in the budget to bring in Krystian Bielik on a deal which could have reached as much as £10m with all add-ons included.

Lampard would soon be named the new manager of Chelsea and, with him, Mason Mount and Fikayo Tomori, two loan stars of the previous season, would return to

Stamford Bridge. The process was long and arduous, and the worst-kept secret in football. Once Chelsea made their interest in Lampard official, their former icon clearly wanted to return to the club with which he had had the most success on the pitch to see if he could replicate it in the dugout. But Morris was not a charity and while he himself loved the nice story of it all, the price still had to be right. Weeks of negotiations commenced with Morris refusing to budge on his compensation price of £4m. And while in the end he got it, one could argue it set the club back, as, when the players all returned for pre-season in Florida, they still had no manager – and the new man would have to fly from the Netherlands to London to Derby and, mercifully, to Florida.

The other outstanding borrowed talent to return to where he came from was Liverpool's Harry Wilson – who Derby did try to bring back for a second loan spell, but the price was too steep. Wilson could blow hot and cold. A streak of six goals in seven games would be followed by no goals or assists in ten – one such sequence also coincided with the team's worst run of the season. Derby was a test for the 20-year-old, not so much for his future there, but more so for what future he had at Liverpool the following season. Could he provide adequate cover for Mohamed Salah, Sadio Mané and Roberto Firmino? Wilson's spell at Derby was excellent – 18 goals and six assists in all competitions. But the number of games he truly dominated rather than decorated could probably be counted on one hand, and he could often bail out an average performance with a showstopping set piece. Nevertheless, he too departed after just one season.

With all of the outgoings, some incomings had to be made quickly. Waiting in the wings to sit in Lampard's dugout seat was former Barcelona captain and 100-cap Netherlands international midfielder Phillip Cocu. Cocu's reputation was bruised following his sacking by Fenerbahçe in October 2018 after just four months in charge of the Turkish giants. Fenerbahçe were undergoing somewhat of an image change after a takeover and new chairman Ali Koç wanted the man who brought so much success to PSV Eindhoven and saw them as Ajax's great conquerors to bring some of that stardust to the Süper Lig and break up its monopolisation by Beşiktaş and Galatasaray. However, just four months into a three-year contract Cocu was sacked, with the club just one point and one place above the relegation zone.

Prior to that unremarkable stint, Cocu had captured three Eredivisie titles in four seasons as manager of PSV and oversaw the development of a clutch of young stars including Georginio Wijnaldum, Steven Bergwijn, Memphis Depay, Davy Pröpper and Hirving Lozano. Morris was banking on Cocu's time in Turkey being more an outlier rather than a true reflection of his coaching abilities. Plus, with a CV that included the development of such young players into talent stars on the world stage, Morris believed Cocu was the perfect foil to steer Derby away from big-money signings and into a more homegrown squad, such was his desire to see a return on his £30m investment into the club's academy.

Morris courted Cocu strongly. The pair met in a London hotel shortly after it was apparent that Lampard would be leaving for pastures new, and they talked football for nearly three hours, during which time Morris became enthralled that Cocu's football philosophy lined up with what he had said he wanted to achieve for Derby going forward – attractive, possession-based performances with the lion's share of the squad made up from academy graduates.

'We could see straight away there was a connection with Phillip, and his assistant manager, Chris [van der Weerden]. What really impressed us was that they weren't just talking about their philosophy and the match was uncannily similar,' Morris told RamsTV of the Cocu hiring in 2019. 'The style of play, the inclusion of younger players in the mix. As the meeting went on we could see they weren't just talking about these things but it's what they do.'

Richard Keogh also pointed to the use of sports science – not uncommon in modern sport, but for some Derby players it was a slightly newer thing to how it had been used under Lampard: 'Being a world-class player and being at Barcelona for a long time, working with the Dutch national team – he's very technical and tactical and a lot of the sessions have been trying to find solutions to different problems. He's taught me things which I see differently in football.'

Cocu was in no hurry to return to coaching and had several offers from the UK and abroad to continue his managerial career. The brief spell at Fenerbahçe made him think twice before taking any job. In hindsight, he believed heading to Turkey was a mistake. A new owner with big ambitions who wanted to take the club in a radical new direction was not for him. He was a manager of evolution, not revolution. And it seemed Morris wanted the same thing – for Derby to evolve from a club that spent big into a club which developed its own players and spent smart.

Perhaps all the noises about wanting to nurture younger players and have the first-team squad brimming with them was, in hindsight, a red flag as to how bad Derby's finances would become and an indicator of the need to cut back on spending in whatever areas the club could. But one could also argue it made sense. Any businessperson investing so heavily in one aspect of their business will, ultimately, wish to see a return on that investment. Morris had overseen Derby's biggest transformation yet behind the scenes, when it came to the academy and the training ground as a whole.

A quick trip around Moor Farm was all it took to realise the club's facilities were at an elite level. Some would often ask, 'What do we need 17 training pitches for?' but the answer was quite simple – it qualified Derby for tier one status as an academy and training ground. The highest there could be.

Max Bird, Jason Knight, Lee Buchanan, Archie Brown, Morgan Whittaker, Eiran Cashin and Louie Sibley highlighted a star-studded under-18s team which romped to the U18 Premier League title following a 5-2 thumping of Arsenal in the final. Some had seen a smattering of first-team training sessions and appearances from the bench under Lampard, but it was now time to give them more minutes in the senior squad under Cocu. The gaps which could not be filled in the transfer market would have to be filled internally – a formula which would put a huge strain on the club the worse the finances got over the coming months. But for the time being, the message was one of sustainability and safeguarding the club's future.

Cocu would officially be hired on 5 July 2019 on a four-year contract believed to be worth in the region of £3m a year. With him came his two loyal assistants – Chris van der Weerden as assistant manager, and Twan Scheepers as a first-team coach. The pair formed an interesting foil around the usually reserved Cocu in that Van der Weerden was himself a tall, dark-haired, mild-mannered individual while Scheepers had long, flowing, blond hair and could often be seen playing air guitar on matchdays whenever Black Sabbath or Motörhead blared over the speakers. He was bombastic and brash and players grew to love him.

There was just one small problem – Derby's pre-season was beginning in earnest in Florida, and neither Cocu nor his assistant were there to oversee any of it.

'I signed for Derby and Frank [Lampard] was a massive part of me wanting to sign here and wanting to play for him,' midfielder Graeme Shinnie, a summer 2019 free transfer from Aberdeen, said during an interview with The Athletic. 'Then coming down and Lampard leaving – then coming into the first day of training with no manager in the building was such a strange feeling. I was a new face around the training ground and it was a weird vibe in general and one I've not been used to. Then the new manager came in and I felt everybody was in the same boat trying to impress him.'

'It was a bit of a strange pre-season. We went in on the first day and we had no manager. So we just did a lot of running in that first session. The academy coaches took the session,' Max Bird told The Athletic in June 2020. 'We didn't really know what was going on in the off-season. We didn't know if we'd come back to a manager or not. Then we went out to Florida and the manager met us there – which is completely different to what's usually done.'

Not only was Cocu not there, it is believed he was not best pleased at having to undertake a pre-season in which he had no say in organising. Nevertheless, he and his team headed over to the US to press on with their preparation. Meanwhile, back at Moor Farm, plans were being made for the new manager and his staff. Cocu had the dynamics of the office spaces changed, with an interconnecting door between his office and that of the academy manager to create a more inclusive feel, but also to keep a close eye on the younger talents.

Academy staff marvelled at how involved Cocu, Scheepers and Van der Weerden were with all the youth squads. Scheepers could often be seen attending the academy games, even in the dugout for many, and would report back to Cocu with his assessments after the fact.

'We've had more meetings between the first team and the academy than we've ever had during my time at the club. We actually played his PSV youth team a couple of years ago … we beat them,' a smiling academy director Darren Wassall said just six weeks after Cocu took over as manager. 'Phillip is really, really into development and growth. He's very clear what he wanted. He comes from a youth development background.

'These changes and the development doesn't happen overnight. It's a fine balancing act between being too busy between the groups, and just letting the young lads develop. But on a daily basis, the academy boys are training with the senior group and for us that's amazing. In the past we've had it whereby academy players would get a session here and there with the first-team lads, which is great, but it never really gave them any consistency, or some managers never got to see all the lads because they wouldn't have them as part of the group. Phillip wants to get all the academy lads mixing in with the first team and it's all about creating one club without any fractures between teams.'

Training was intense when Cocu arrived in the States. He immediately set to work on getting the squad up to speed with the level of technique he demanded from his players, and many struggled to begin with.

'The one that I recall the most was when we were in Florida, we played a lot of possession games,' Bird recalled in an interview with The Athletic. 'Somebody would kick the ball above head height and the whistle would go – he wanted the ball on the floor. A lot of the possession drills we'd have in triangle shapes, we'd do four against two in a box, one-touch stuff and move and create angles. At the start we couldn't really do it. But just before the [Covid] lockdown happened we were brilliant at it. Some of us thought it was a hard drill and that we'd never be able to do it but we've all developed as a group.'

Cocu wanted his team to play aggressively off the ball and press high up the pitch. If the opportunity to press did not present itself, he insisted on a compact shape in the middle to squeeze the opposition to the outside and limit their options in attack.

When on the ball, Cocu believed in a balance of structure and creativity to help create openings but also mitigate against opposition counterattacks.

'I believe in setting up until the final third, more or less, and from the final third you can create,' he told The Athletic in September 2020. 'You can sometimes train an overlap or a switch but the intuition of a striker to make a run or a dribble is their call, it's why they're in that position. It's their quality. Use it.'

Cocu also believed in creating overloads down the flanks to outnumber defenders, a typically Dutch tradition of football which, as the game itself has become more global, has been tweaked to reinvent it many times over. But, at its core, Cocu wanted to use it to provide Derby with advantages, open up running lanes and give opposition defenders problems when trying to make decisions.

'It's like a chain reaction,' Cocu told The Athletic in September 2021. 'When you have three against two, and then the next player also runs into the back of the defence and, by using a striker [dropping deep], then the winger makes a run beyond, it's like you're not creating only in midfield but you're creative to be able to go into the final third. It's something we use a lot in training and something we focus on because a lot of teams play quite deep so if you didn't take the initiative to come out of smaller areas it was very hard to create.'

Those overloads were to be supplemented by positional switches. Again a staple of Dutch football, popularised by Johan Cruyff, Cocu believed that players should be comfortable in several positions and could use rotations to drag their markers out of position, which then runners could exploit. But he knew mastering such skills would take time.

'It takes a lot [of work] because it's about understanding between the players,' he said. 'To be dynamic and to rotate and take over positions cannot be a casual coincidence that it happens and you score a goal.

'I like it because if you're static you get predictable, then you really need so much individual quality to create and score. So if you're able to change position and make the opponent change and come out of their zone, you open up spaces and you can be more creative and a lot of players participate in the process.'

Of course, the positional switching wouldn't work if Cocu had players who were only specialists in one area. Thankfully the squad featured several flexible players such as Duane Holmes, Tom Lawrence, Martyn Waghorn and Jason Knight, and he would also bring in Krystian Bielik to assist with that, while Wayne Rooney would of course later join the fold.

Cocu emphasised the ability to play multiple positions. It was not only good for the team, but it was good for the individual too, as they might see more minutes based on the fact they can cover more areas, 'I think it makes you a more complete player. But in some positions you need a specialist who can make the difference. You need a combination of specialists in certain positions but also players who you can use in different positions are important in a team. The understanding of the game gets so much better because you play in all these different positions.

'It might not be his favourite one but if he believes he can play well for the team then it's important. So you have to have a dialogue and sit down with the player and talk about what is expected from him in that position, then they can enjoy themselves. But you have to be clear in your message as a coach what is expected as a player. You need to have the physical profile to fit in, you need the tactical awareness to execute the job, the player has to believe in the position.'

Within the squad, Cocu had several players already who he believed could carry out such versatile jobs. Lawrence would often flit from inverted left-winger to number ten, and to a false nine at times. Waghorn would do the same jobs on the opposite wing. Striker Chris Martin would be less versatile but would still be used as an extra central midfielder to link play when dropping deep; meanwhile a deeper central midfielder would gallop forwards to fill the centre-forward space which Martin had vacated.

Perhaps no two players signified Cocu's wish for versatility more than Holmes and Knight. The pair were similar, with some notable differences. In the academy setup Knight was part of a fearsome central midfielder duo with Bird in which the Irishman netted eight goals and laid on four assists in all youth competitions. However, with the centre of the park well stocked at senior level, Knight had to settle for more of a Swiss Army knife role – often playing a more defensive winger, but sometimes popping up as the number ten; he even had stints at right-back when required. The same could be said for Holmes. He had spoken with Cocu and told him of his desire to play as a number ten – Cocu retorted with a harsh assessment of Holmes, however, declaring he did not believe the US international was fit enough to carry out such a role on a full-time basis. As a result, the nippy, tenacious midfielder also had to settle for a do-it-all role in the squad, also playing at right-back, central midfield, on the right wing and, on occasion, as a number ten. In total both Knight and Holmes each played in five separate positions during Cocu's first season – partly due to necessity with a shallow squad constantly besotted by injury, but partly also down to the Dutch manager's insistence that players be multiple in their uses for the team.

However, Cocu still felt more versatility was required and he set about finding some more players who fit a certain profile and could be versatile enough to carry out the ideals he clearly held in such high regards. The process was harmed by a lacklustre first transfer window.

Alongside Bielik, for an initial fee believed to be around £7.5 million and potentially rising to £10 million, attacker Jamie Paterson, playmaker Kieran Dowell and goalkeeper Ben Hamer all arrived on loan.

Bielik was the headline act of the bunch. The Polish international was thought of highly by Arsène Wenger at Arsenal and had previously enjoyed a good spell at Charlton Athletic, but then manager Lee Bowyer did have some concerns about the midfielder's fitness back then – indicating that Bielik would be good to miss at least ten games a season with niggling injuries. Nevertheless, Derby had snagged themselves an ascending young player with a high resale value if he was to hit his ceiling. And Bielik was ambitious, too. He had stated that if he was not playing in the Premier League within five years of him signing for Derby, he would consider it a huge failure.

Bielik also fit the profile of player Cocu was courting – a silky technician with the ability to dictate play from deep, but also with the versatility to play multiple positions.

Cocu initially played Bielik as a centre-back, as he found his way back to fitness after an early shoulder injury, but would later revert to playing him as a deep midfielder allowing the playmaker to dictate the tempo of the team. There was still, though, a big belief that Cocu would open up his contacts book and bring in players he knew well from his time in the Netherlands. In fact it was one of the reasons for which Derby fans became increasingly excited by his hiring. Lampard had flexed his muscles to bring in players from his former clubs and leveraged great relationships he had in the industry; so would Cocu be making Derby County a Total Football side with a healthy smattering of Dutch distinction? To much bemusement, that did not prove to be the case. In fact Cocu was rather frosty when quizzed about his relationships with former clubs.

During his introductory press conference, Cocu was frosty and tight-lipped as to whether he would be ringing some old friends from PSV to take advantage of his connections and some of their budding stars with friendly loan deals, much like his predecessor had done. Cocu had made it clear that he would not be bringing in any of his former players and when pressed as to why he simply responded, 'Yes, there is a reason.' His demeanour until that point had been charming, full of smiles, warm eye-contact and glowing praise for his new employers. Yet the seemingly natural question about whether Cocu was going to leverage his past relationships brought a stonier gaze and a cold response designed to shut down any follow-up questions, and indeed the question disappeared almost as quickly as it had arrived.

Instead Derby settled for what they could get in the quick turnaround since Cocu had arrived and also being tighter with the purse strings.

Both Dowell and Paterson quickly fizzled out. The duo played just ten games each. In the case of the former, he started the first six matches of the season but after a particularly bruising 3-0 defeat away to Brentford at the end of August he would be dropped. It is believed Cocu would later privately proclaim that he 'didn't see it' in the midfielder, leading some to believe that the new boss was not all that involved with some of the recruitment process, save for Bielik whom he had identified and pushed hard for.

Dowell had arrived on loan from Everton after a middling second-half-of-the-season stint at Sheffield United in 2018/19. It was Derby's hope that he could fill the void left by Mason Mount, but he struggled to settle in and, while Cocu had reservations about his new signing, internally the players were left surprised that a player of such technical quality was being left out so consistently and puzzled as to why Cocu could not get the best out of him.

The same could be said of Paterson. After having an unconvincing season at Bristol City, the attacking midfielder was recruited in a bid to fill the Harry Wilson-shaped hole. He struggled mightily to even get minutes, often limited to substitute appearances for just 15 minutes here and there. However, his assist for a dramatic leveller against Leeds United at Elland Road was enough to propel him into the starting XI where he showed good chemistry with Chris Martin. It wasn't enough for Cocu, and Paterson's loan was also terminated and he returned to Bristol City, where he would become one of their

best players throughout the second half of the season –
naturally.

If those signings were lukewarm at best, the next one
was about to rock the entire football landscape.

2

He Goes by the Name of Wayne Rooney

WHILE STILL riding the wave of the club spending big on Krystian Bielik, Derby fans were hit with a tsunami: Wayne Rooney was to sign. There is no way to build it up any more than that really. He really was signing for Derby County, in a plot twist so bizarre that Twitter was convinced humanity had been sucked into a *Football Manager* save. If the end of the previous season had taken all the wind out of Derby's sails, Mel Morris was determined to get the spirits picked up and momentum in full swing as quickly as possible.

Rumblings of the transfer spread throughout social media, the press box and the away end at Derby's opening match of 2019/20, a Monday night trip to Huddersfield Town – even the home supporters had a waft that something unusual was afoot. And by half-time, with journalists swivelling their heads towards each other asking if they had seen this report and that report, desperately searching for Morris's bald head in the crowd to quiz him on the insanity, Derby fans were at fever pitch.

Morris was grinning from ear to ear at the back of the executive box as the story circulated around stunned media in the press box and disbelieving fans in the stadium. The atmosphere had shifted – that Derby went into the break 2-1 up in Cocu's first game in charge through two stunning Tom Lawrence goals was the icing on the cake, but in truth nobody really cared. Morris refused to engage with journalists and fans passing by, asking if what they were reading and hearing was true. He wasn't able to comment, so he said, but his toothy grin told a whole different story. The move was kept so in the dark that even many of the club's communications staff didn't have a clue as to what was happening. Journalists desperately tried to collar somebody in a Derby County-branded jacket but they were equally scrambling to put the pieces together in the belly of the John Smith's Stadium.

Even some of the players thought the news was fake. 'For the team everybody was in shock, and in awe. Everybody was a bit nervous that he was actually here,' said Max Bird in June 2020. 'It didn't really sink in for a while that I was playing with him and training with him. I was thinking, "Wow, I'm actually training with Wayne Rooney here." He has been brilliant with the team. He's been very helpful on and off the pitch.'

After the game Cocu marched into the press room with pace and a neutral look on his face; one could assume that the press officer had briefed him to expect a lot of Wayne Rooney questions – and he got them. Of course there was the usual politeness of, 'So Phillip, first win as Derby County manager, how does that feel?' and the odd, 'Were you encouraged by how the players implemented your style of play?' But really, all anybody wanted to know was whether Wayne Rooney was signing for the club.

If Morris wasn't briefing the press, what other choice did Cocu have? He was tight-lipped and stoic, giving flocking journalists the regulation responses when it comes to transfer rumours, 'At the moment I can't say anything. I cannot say anything about names before things are done. We have a lot of players we think could be an asset for the team. You always try to get the best you can with the resources at the club. A few more days then hopefully I can say something more.'

It was a response and gave little in the way of a juicy update on the scenario. However, in future transfer windows Cocu would go into a touch more detail when it came to players he was courting – perhaps in hindsight his saying nothing on the Rooney situation said an awful lot.

He would be afforded to say more the very next day. On 6 August Wayne Rooney would be unveiled as a Derby player. He really was joining. The scenes outside Pride Park were ones of chaos. ITV, Sky Sports, the BBC and any other media company with a truck pulled up outside Pride Park Stadium. Inside, a usually spacious press room was as tight as a sardine can. A full row of cameras was set up about 15ft away from the podium Rooney would speak from, and up front photographers gathered, crouching down with their fingers on the trigger waiting for the door to swing open and Manchester United's all-time top goalscorer to appear. The air was populated by the rattling of keyboards from written reporters and broadcast journalists going through sound checks. The room froze with every creak of a door hinge – and the ensuing disappointment when it was just the tea lady, or somebody returning from a hasty trip to the toilet, only made the euphoria when he appeared all the sweeter. Derby even drafted in another more senior communications specialist to handle the media frenzy which had accompanied Rooney's arrival. Such an occasion required decorum – broadcast journalists first, led of course by Sky Sports – then written press later. But with every answer Rooney gave to a question, thumbs and fingers went into turbo, tweeting and typing his every utterance, canvassing his every expression to see what really lay behind the words being spoken.

Derby would have to wait patiently, however. Signing on an initial 18-month contract as a player-coach, Rooney would return to MLS side DC United to complete his obligations before linking up with the Rams in January 2020 to help boost, what he hoped, would be a play-off charge.

'Obviously my agent spoke to the club and the owners here. There was a deal which could happen and I had a decision to make, and the opportunity to come back to England and play, but also to work with Phillip, was too great for me to turn down,' Rooney said during his unveiling. 'Firstly I'm a player. I feel I've got a lot of quality I can bring to the squad. Secondly I want to try and learn off Phillip and his staff to gain experience for when I do stop playing and take that next step. I spoke with Phillip on the phone to see what the situation was with him. It's important to get the manager's opinion.'

Publicly, Cocu was also thrilled, 'It's a great signing for the club and for the team. A player with his quality, his experience is absolutely an asset for the club. Also the way we work, develop the youngsters, so he can help the team to develop and we can help him in the future role as being a coach and being a manager – it's a perfect moment to join together.'

However, privately there were some questions as to whether Cocu had much say in the Rooney signing, or if Morris had spotted an opportunity and it had been too good to turn down – not just from a player standpoint, but in terms of marketing the club as well. Those concerns only became apparent after a little while of Rooney and Cocu being in close proximity to each other. The pair were described as awkward around each other – cordial, certainly. But something just wasn't right.

There were question marks as to how Derby facilitated such a deal, too. Derby had already dug deep to sign Bielik even after Morris had previously hinted at tighter purse strings during Cocu's introductory press conference just a couple of weeks prior. Rooney would technically come on a free transfer, but he would not be playing for free. His wages would command a hefty portion of Derby's outgoings. If players such as Martyn Waghorn, Richard Keogh and Tom Lawrence were touching close to a reported £30,000 a week, it was safe to assume that Rooney would be earning double that – at least.

Eyebrows were also raised at Rooney wearing the number 32 shirt. Derby's sponsors were betting company 32Red and reports suggested that they would be footing a large chunk of the bill so, as part of their deal, Rooney would don the number 32, an allegation he dismissed.

It is believed that Morris had activated a 'star player' clause in the sponsorship deal with 32Red which meant the gambling giant handed over an extra £1.5m to the club in one lump sum. Derby also activated the deal when Frank Lampard became manager and, in turn, it allowed 32Red to increase their investment into the club and also gave the sponsor more opportunities to interview Lampard for their own content streams.

Although plenty of reports suggested 32Red were paying Rooney's wages, the sponsor insisted that was not the case. 'We're not paying his wages, reports that we're contributing 80 per cent of his wages ... it's nowhere near that,' said Tom Banks of 32Red. 'The total sponsorship is about £2m a year for the sponsorship on the front of the shirt. It's increased to around £3.5m with the star players clause – it's about ten weeks of his wages, it's nowhere near the reporting of what it was. And it's not even necessarily touching the sides of the FFP argument. Now of course it does help, but it's not clearing any debt for them to sign him completely. It's just additional money. It's not a deal with Wayne Rooney, it's a deal with Derby. All 32Red have done is paid a bit more in their sponsorship agreement to get more access to Rooney.

'We accept that some of the reporting was partly because we hadn't got on the front foot and said all of this straight away. I think we were a bit overwhelmed. So then we had to tell people how this deal worked. But it got whipped up so quickly that we thought to let it ride and respond when we can.

'What was part of the agreement – things like him taking the number 32 and stuff, that was a club decision to do that. It wasn't a stipulation of the deal. For transparency, as part of any star player agreement the shirt number was one of the things on there that we could potentially get as part of any deal, alongside training ground naming rights or other bits. There was a long list of things on there and Derby decided to go with the shirt number. But when the number on his shirt was 32, I think it got whipped up that he would be a billboard. We don't have a trademark on the number 32, it's not a trademark it's just a number. There were concerns about the kids' shirts and having gambling sponsors on the front of the number 32 and Rooney's name on the back but there is actually no factual or statistical evidence to suggest that a number 32 on the back increases any chances of gambling.'

Reports suggested that 32Red knew about the deal well ahead of time, and had played a major role in getting Rooney to Derby, but the company denied the claims and insisted that they did not know about the deal until Derby were ready to announce it and only got in touch to activate the 'star player' clause once more.

It is believed that the clause was also offered to be triggered when Derby signed former Arsenal, Chelsea and England left-back Ashley Cole but the club turned it down due to Cole's standing in the game diminishing by the time he joined the Rams in January 2019. The parameters for the clause were loose. A player needing to have earned a certain number of caps for their country and having won a certain number of trophies were among other vague specifications. As part of the deal, 32Red were given exclusive time with Rooney for their content as well as the former England captain appearing in a series of anti-gambling videos, and they also invested more in the community.

'32Red in terms of its investment into Derby, they invested in a men's mental health scheme that the

Community Trust run called Team Talk,' said Banks. 'Back in February [2019] before any of this Rooney business came about, we tweaked our sponsorship deals to make sure they benefit the community as well. 32Red also invested about ten per cent of their sponsorship agreement, on top of their deal, into this project. It was initially just a pilot scheme being run out of Derby's Community Trust office, and now there are five centres across the city and it'll get hundreds of men involved over the next 18 months and enable them to talk about their mental health with other Derby fans.'

The other rumour which refused to dissipate was that Rooney had been promised the manager's job – and that it was a prerequisite for him signing. Rooney had never made any bones about wanting to become a manager, but of course finding that first job may have proved a challenge in a competitive landscape – and it was hard to envisage Rooney starting his managerial career in non-league or even League Two for that matter. In an even more bizarre twist, some had speculated that Richard Keogh was in line to be Rooney's assistant when the time came for the torch to be passed – with Keogh even supposedly having discussed the matter with Morris upon Rooney's arrival. But for now it was all just rumours, no matter how strong.

Rooney's signing was a two-pronged approach; not only was it to boost the team on the field, his name recognition was there to boost the stature of the club off the field too. And it worked. Social media numbers, shirt sales and attendances all spiked within a month of him joining properly in January.

The initial tweet announcing Rooney garnered 4.7 million impressions. During the following 24 hours, the club's Rooney-related tweets got 7.6 million impressions in total. Derby's Instagram following also received a boom in its numbers. Solely on the day Rooney was announced, 20,000 people chose to follow the club's official account. Across all social media platforms, a total of 26,700 new followers signed up. The YouTube highlights from Rooney's debut, a 2-1 home victory over Barnsley in January 2020, uploaded to Derby's official channel, were watched more than 70,000 times in its first month.

It was the impact Morris knew would take effect with such an icon joining his club, and he did not shy away from wanting more eyes on Derby County – especially as he was increasingly looking to sell up. Rooney was the main man for every interview, the frontman for every picture in the club shop. Every bit of content or merchandise that needed selling – Rooney was the man to market it along with a couple of other high-profile players.

Attendances were also up – hovering around 27,000 until football was locked down with the rest of the world in March 2020 following the start of the Covid-19 pandemic – and shirt sales had risen by 30 per cent. Not all of that was down to Rooney shirts flying off the rack but he did account for a large swathe of them leaving the megastore.

The transfer was even dictating which matches would be covered on television. An otherwise unremarkable game between Derby and Barnsley on New Year's Day was suddenly moved by Sky Sports to a day later when it could take up a prime-time slot in the evening. All in all, the Rooney experiment seemed to be working – and he'd not even set foot on the football pitch yet. His impact would not be felt until January. Between August and the new year, Derby's season would peak and trough in a volatile manner.

3

A Night of Madness

PHILLIP COCU had been at the helm for a couple of months when he decided to organise a team-bonding day between all the senior squad and playing staff. The move drew a mixed reaction from fans – who believed having seen the club make an inauspicious start to the Championship season, winning just one game, drawing five and losing two, such an idea was a sign of the manager already battling to keep the dressing room happy. However, in reality it made more sense in the context of Cocu having arrived late in pre-season, not really having time to know the players – both existing and new acquisitions – and the club had a nice international break coming up to breathe a little and for Cocu and his staff to bond further with the squad, and for the group to know what made their new coaching staff tick.

The original plan was to play footgolf or even paintball, but the rainy weather made both activities a non-starter. So, instead, tenpin bowling was the call followed by a meal at a pub in nearby Quarndon. It all seemed rather straightforward. However, what was to follow would start one of the rockiest subplots of Derby's entire season.

On 24 September 2019, after a team-bonding session of bowling and a meal at the Joiner's Arms, an ambulance, passing by chance, would find a smashed-up Range Rover with Derby captain Richard Keogh unconscious inside. He had been involved in a terrible drink-driving accident along with team-mates Tom Lawrence and Mason Bennett, both of whom fled the scene initially and then returned around 45 minutes later, by which time Keogh had already headed home having convinced the passing paramedics not to take him to the hospital where he would no doubt be recognised, as revealed during the court hearing in October.

Keogh started off walking before a police car gave him a lift the rest of the way. Bennett, meanwhile, was taken to St Mary's Wharf police station and Lawrence was treated at hospital before later cooperating with the police intoxilyzer process and giving readings.

The club released a statement in the aftermath of the incident, part of which read:

'As a club, we cannot, and do not, condone the actions of a small group of players on Tuesday evening.

'The players were out as part of a scheduled team-building dinner with staff and while the majority of them acted responsibly and left at around 8pm and were not involved, a small group, including the team captain Richard Keogh, continued drinking into the night. They should have known when to stop and also ignored the opportunity to be driven home using cars laid on by the club, and chose to stay out.'

The last line about the club laying taxis on for the players was a curious one for many of the squad who read the statement.

'We all drove there,' young defender Max Lowe said. 'There were no taxis. We all drove there and the expectation was we were all going to drive home. I've no idea why the club put in the statement that there were taxis. I'm categorically saying there weren't any taxis arranged for the lads.'

'I remember my wife telling me when I woke up the next day that some of the lads had an accident,' experienced centre-back Curtis Davies recounted. 'I saw it on Sky Sports and then I texted the lads – I didn't know the context of it at the time. Once I caught more wind of it I offered my support.'

'I was staying at Centre Parcs with Jack [Marriott],' Duane Holmes continued. 'We left at about seven o'clock and a few lads stayed behind for some drinks but it was nothing crazy when we left. When I woke up the next day I'd still not heard anything about it.'

There was no such inquest at the training ground that morning, but the players were understandably shocked at what had happened the night before and spent large parts of the day wondering what had led them to this moment.

'Then it became a task of trying to piece together the story. The story seemed never-ending. Other snippets were coming out of the woodwork all the time,' Davies continued. 'I'd gone home long before they left. It was only the local lads who were still there but not everybody was involved in it. Then we learned the fact that Richard had done his knee and smashed his hand up. It was difficult. It was crazy. I was so glad that something more serious didn't happen.

'It became like telling your kids off almost – you're still going to love the lads, I've gone to war with these guys on the pitch. But you're so disappointed in what they've done. And you knew there was going to be a lot of trouble for them lads and I was trying to make them understand and accept that – and they did. I'm not trying to dust over it at all.

'I remember being at a Community Trust thing with Mel, and I was sitting at his table. Usually the players leave at about 9.30. I was there until 11. It was all about putting a front on, showing we have good people at the club. Saving the reputation of the club. It also ended up being that, politically, I started the game against Birmingham, which we won 3-2. I think the fact that they needed a leader on the pitch, having been through a lot with the club up to that point, I think the club needed that visibility.'

The fall-out was seismic. The squad did not find out the full extent of the incident until they came into training the day after and were told by Cocu and Mel Morris. The reaction was a stunned silence, before the players were expected to go out and train for a match against Birmingham City at Pride Park.

'I found out when I got to training and I saw Rich there on crutches – and I noticed he had a black eye,' Holmes said. 'I thought he'd got into a fight or something. Tom and Mason weren't there the next day, they didn't return to training until the day after so it was all really strange. I remember Mel telling us all that Richard was like a son to him, and how things are going to be OK and all of that – it still didn't compute what had happened though. Why did they drive? They didn't live that far away. I didn't understand why they drove home. My first initial thought was, "Are Tom and Mason OK?" because I'd seen the state that Richard was in and I wanted to know where Tom and Mason were.'

Keogh had not seen or heard from either Lawrence or Bennett at that point in time but was asking after them, concerned about their health and if anything potentially serious had happened to his team-mates.

Keogh sustained a torn ACL, a wrist injury and several head and facial injuries. There was a worry his career was over and there were further questions over the futures of Lawrence and Bennett. There were calls from some fans and media for the pair to be sacked for their actions.

Before that hearing could be reached though, Derby had games to play and went into crisis PR mode to manage the situation. Morris met with supporters in the cafe located at the stadium prior to kick-off against Birmingham City. He apologised to those in attendance and explained the situation would be dealt with seriously but the club could not communicate much due to the ongoing investigation. After that, he was marching towards the South Stand and waving to the stands along with Cocu and placing his arm around the Dutch manager. The pictures showed solidarity, strength, support and a bid to control the message that Derby County was bigger than the awful incident.

Derby went on to beat Birmingham 3-2 in dramatic fashion to provide a much-needed tonic to the midweek events.

Amid the turmoil was who would be captain in Keogh's absence. Tom Huddlestone had initially been given the armband after what became known as 'Joinersgate' but was promptly stripped of it when a video emerged from his private Snapchat account of Bennett vomiting into a urinal. Off camera, several people could be heard joking that Bennett was going to vomit again, that three pints of Peroni was strong and 'get it all out, Mas' while the forward asked for the phones to be put away and reached for tissues.

'That video of Mason that came out from Tom's Snapchat … it's all hindsight,' Davies said. 'Did Tom know that Mason was going to drive? If Tom [Huddlestone] sees Mason walking to his car and stumbling over, then I'd have taken offence at what Tom did. But we've all filmed our mates when they can't handle their drink and you take the mick. Not for one moment did Tom think that Mason was going to drive home in that state.

'It was almost like Tom was taken down with them a bit. But Tom did nothing wrong. He was at home by about 10pm. He filmed a mate, like a lot of us have done, who'd had too much to drink. And his friend made that bad decision. If Tom was there, I don't think Mason gets in his car. But it was a weird situation. And then I think politically I had to be the captain after that because I can front up on the pitch because I'm bold enough. But also off the pitch I would be the only spokesperson to say anything because I'm quite controlled in what I can say. I think that got me the captaincy more than the manager actually giving it me because he believed I'd play every game.'

Morris had asked the players in a meeting he held after the incident if there was anything else that happened that could be leaked to the press so the club could get ahead of the story and plan their next moves accordingly, but no players came forward.

The trio had left the Joiner's Arms at around 11.30pm to go home. While driving, Lawrence's car smashed into the back of Bennett's before continuing across a roundabout and hitting 'street furniture', the subsequent court hearing was told.

However, according to the statement released from the club in the aftermath of the incident, they claimed to have laid on taxis to take the players home, specifically to avoid any member of staff or the squad from drink-driving.

It was a rainy and bitterly cold morning on 15 October when flocks of media gathered outside Southern Derbyshire Magistrates' Court to await the arrival of Lawrence and Bennett for their hearing. The pair arrived shortly after 9am dressed in black suits and were ushered into the building by security as smatterings of camera flashes greeted them. They looked straight at the floor as they walked in, not raising their heads once, a trend which would continue throughout the hearing taking place in Court 1. The duo entered guilty pleas to driving with excess alcohol and failing to stop at an accident.

The court heard that Welsh international Lawrence, 25, gave a breath test reading of 58mcg per 100ml and Bennett a reading of 64. The legal limit is 35mcg per 100ml.

The hearing was told that Lawrence was drinking alcohol as a means to boost his confidence and as a way to deal with his grief of losing his mother, Deborah, at the tail end of the 2018/19 season, and that he was 'quite dependent' upon alcohol. Derby had organised counselling to help aid his grieving. Then Wales manager Ryan Giggs gave Lawrence a glowing character reference in the hearing, as did former Derby manager Frank Lampard. Shaun Draycott, representing Lawrence, said the references testified to Lawrence being a 'decent young man who behaved out of character'.

Draycott also added, 'What he [Lawrence] did was wrong, was serious,' adding that his client made a 'gross error of judgement'.

For Bennett's defence, Lucy Whitaker told the court that Lawrence regretted his actions and explained away the drinking to the point of vomiting, 'He accepts he had some alcohol at that point and consumed a Jägerbomb that was bought for him which made him sick.

'It wasn't bought by him, but from a team-mate. He didn't want it but felt peer-pressured to have it.'

Ms Whitaker revealed to the court that Bennett planned to get a taxi home but made the 'poor decision' to drive instead – stating that he lived three miles away from the pub.

In the immediate aftermath of the crash, the court heard how Bennett panicked and drove away from the scene with another team-mate – who was not named – in the car before receiving a phone call from Lawrence asking Bennett to pick him up from a nearby garage.

Bennett's defence also revealed that the Derby academy graduate was upset at the prospect of custody because of his four-year-old daughter – to whom the court heard he was a caring and responsible father.

District judge Jonathan Taaffe was scathing in his assessment of both Lawrence and Bennett as the pair rose to their feet to hear the verdicts after a two-hour hearing, warning them that they had been very lucky to escape a prison sentence or a fate much worse.

'You are intelligent and talented young men who brought shame upon yourselves, your families, your profession and your club,' Mr Taaffe said. 'Those who pay hard-earned money to watch you play regard you as role models, very well-paid role models. Many will be incredulous that professional athletes, during the season, on a so-called team-bonding day, are drinking and then making a decision to drive. You may struggle to accept this but you are extremely fortunate to be here today.

'The aggravated features of the matter are many: drinking, choosing to drive when clearly there was no need to do so, an accident between two vehicles in unexplained circumstances, leaving the scene when a fellow professional was injured in the back of one of those vehicles. Some would say you did so out of panic, some would say you did so to save your own skin after realising the magnitude of what had occurred.'

Mr Taaffe did, however, give the pair a smidgen of credit before handing down their sentences, highlighting them returning to the scene, their good character, the accident being an isolated incident and cooperating with the police, before adding:

'The readings before me in terms of drink-driving are not the highest. The fact that you are professional footballers in my view doesn't mean you should be treated any differently to anyone else who appears before this court. I don't intend to treat you any differently as you are professional footballers. In both cases, the same sentence will be imposed.'

The ruling was a two-year driving ban for both players, along with 12-month community orders, being ordered to carry out 180 hours of unpaid community service, and paying costs of £85 and a £90 victim surcharge.

In addition, the club had fined them both six weeks' wages and ordered them to 80 hours of community service, both seen as the maximum possible punishments. Lawrence and Bennett completed their court-ordered community service first before undertaking the 80 hours handed down by the club.

After a brief moment out of the spotlight, Lawrence and Bennett returned for the following match, a 2-2 draw against Barnsley, to a very mixed response. In an ideal world both would have had extended spells away from the club – to protect them from the inevitable reactions if nothing else. But Cocu was already in a position whereby he was trying to gain some momentum, the squad was looking thin due to injuries, and in Lawrence's case Cocu needed one of his best players to give a performance. But the whole scenario was hardly ideal – and the decision to include them in the squad split both fans and players.

'I'm not sure it was the right call,' a source said. 'In one way it was a chance to get their minds off things, try to focus on something else other than the incident and just try to get a bit of normality around them. But the reaction – from some of our own fans too – was brutal. And you can understand why. But also for the boys in the dressing room it had all happened so fast and we wondered if Tom and Mason needed a bit of time away

– where was their head at? Did they maybe need saving from themselves a bit?'

Fans outside Oakwell were equally split, ranging from those wanting Lawrence, Bennett and Keogh sacked to not jumping to conclusions and wanting to hear the results of the court case later in October and going from there. It also caused a moral dilemma among supporters, too. Some felt it was the perfect chance to move Bennett on, a player who had never fulfilled his potential and had never even finished 90 minutes for Derby, but keep Lawrence and Keogh on board. A player with some value and the club captain respectively were assets to any team.

When Lawrence and Bennett had their names read out over the Oakwell tannoy system, they would be met with sizeable boos from all sections of the crowd. Lawrence started the game but Bennett settled for a place on the bench. With every touch of the ball Lawrence had, boos would loudly rain down on him. It became harder and harder to tell where they were coming from. Chants of 'Tom Lawrence, you should be in jail' also greeted him and every time the Welshman went over to take a corner near the Barnsley fans he was met with vicious jeers, hand gestures and outright abuse. His head was down more often than not and the game seemed to swallow him the longer it went on – but Cocu persisted and kept his under-fire winger out there all night.

Bennett, by comparison, came off the bench for just one minute. His name was roundly booed when he was being announced as replacing Duane Holmes, but then a section of Derby fans broke into an encouraging song of 'Mason Bennett, he's one of our own'. Perhaps the mood was uplifted by the fact the Rams were winning at the time, but a last-minute Barnsley equaliser soured the mood and brought with it another strange atmosphere.

After the game, Cocu said the pair were not 'off the hook' but believed the only place they could make amends to the fans and the club was by turning in good performances on the pitch.

Lawrence would continue to be a mainstay in the side but it was obvious he was not at his best, and the mental woes of what had gone on were deeply impacting his performances. Lawrence would score just three goals and lay on one assist in the next 15 games until he was suspended before the turn of the year after picking up too many bookings. A player who could be hit and miss at the best of times, he was even more volatile in his performances in the aftermath of the crash. It wasn't helped by opposition supporters furiously booing him, chanting about him, whistling, swearing and generally making his life unpleasant any time he touched the ball.

The nadir of his treatment by opposition fans came in November's 1-0 defeat to Nottingham Forest – the Remembrance Sunday game – at the City Ground. Lawrence was peppered with chants from the over 20,000 home fans in attendance ranging from 'you should be in jail, Tom Lawrence, you should be in jail' to 'he left him for dead, he left him for dead'. Lawrence was sworn at when lining up to take corners and booed heavily with every touch. The stadium was merciless on him. The torment had become part and parcel of every game since the crash, but the match against Derby's fiercest rivals saw the tension ratchet up to another level.

In the case of Bennett, he would play just 43 more minutes for the club before being loaned out, and later down the line sold, to Millwall. Bennett's progress under Cocu never really got going to begin with, and although he played a vital role in what had happened on that night in September, that he was ushered out of the club with next to no fanfare was representative of how little fans mourned his leaving – even if he was one of their own. While he was on loan at the New Den, he did himself no favours by taking a private Snapchat of himself passing Pride Park and saying 'Burn. Fucking burn' in the direction of Pride Park. Bennett later apologised and said the video was intended as a private joke with a friend, posting, 'The video that's come out was a private joke, didn't mean any harm to the derby fans. The club has been great with me and will always be grateful. I apologise if I've offended anyone. There is a picture of my good friend Shinz [Graeme Shinnie] and it was a joke to him.'

The apology perplexed some within the club, who claimed they had never really seen him interact much with the Scot and did not see them as the good friends Bennett was claiming they were.

'He was a nice guy but … he had no common sense. And I think he was always in with a bad crowd,' Max Lowe said. 'Some of the things he'd say you'd have to laugh, and not even because they were intentionally funny but sometimes he'd just say some unbelievable things which made you think "wow".'

The decision regarding Richard Keogh represented the most controversial call and was one which fractured the club deeply. He was sacked – much to his and everybody else's shock. The former captain was in the stands just days before his dismissal to witness Derby's dramatic 1-0 victory over Wigan Athletic in the pouring rain at Pride Park. Keogh was on crutches in the press box and decked out in his Derby County tracksuit and was seen smiling and laughing; players came up to greet him as did members of the analysis staff who he stood next to as they made their way up to the press box for a more bird's eye view. Even journalists wandered over to greet him and wish him well. The expectation was that Keogh would remain at the club even though he was ruled out for the rest of the season with his injuries.

Days later, however, he was called into a meeting with Morris and had his contract terminated. It is believed Keogh was not even allowed back to the training ground to say his goodbyes to his former team-mates and friends after the decision had been made.

'I'm never going to say I want my friends to be sacked,' Holmes said, referring to Lawrence and Bennett. 'But Richard was our friend – above all else he was our friend. Mel had a meeting with us a couple of days after the incident and told us he was going to look after him, that he thought of Richard like a son.'

Several members of the first-team squad pleaded with Cocu and Morris not to sack Keogh, but the pleas fell on deaf ears as Morris felt he had no option due to 'gross misconduct' and Keogh neglecting his captaincy.

'He was the one least to blame – that was the general feeling in the dressing room. It felt like he got hung out to dry,' Holmes continued. 'I didn't understand how he could get a different punishment to the other two lads. That decision created a weird feeling in the dressing room for a while. Because it felt unfair. And it made it a bit weird in the dressing room. Why did he get sacked? Why couldn't he have been punished similar to Tom and Mason? It didn't sit right with me. We were disappointed with Tom and Mason obviously, but we cared for them as well and wanted them to be OK too and support them. It was just an awful situation.'

'I'm not sitting here saying they all should have been sacked,' Lowe continued. 'But for me the punishment has to go across the board, whatever it is the club decided to do, fines, community service, whatever. It has to be the same for everybody there – and I remember Mel telling us all that he's probably going to have to sack Richard and I was shocked. Why just him? He was silly to get in the car, but obviously he didn't drive drunk. It was a weird decision and it felt like a way to get him off the books because he was one of our highest earners. It created a weird vibe in the dressing room because obviously the lads loved Richard, and we were worried for Tom and Mason.'

There was no ill will towards Bennett or Lawrence within the dressing room. Their team-mates felt more a sense of disappointment than anger but still rallied behind them knowing the mental impact it had on the pair and offered their support accordingly.

Originally the club were willing to keep Keogh on, but requested he take a significant pay cut. When he rejected the offer, Derby sacked him for 'gross misconduct' and said in a statement, 'The club will not tolerate any of its players or staff behaving in a manner which puts themselves, their colleagues, and members of the general public at risk of injury or worse, or which brings the club into disrepute. The club will be making no further comment at this time regards this matter until the conclusion of any potential appeal.'

Keogh did appeal the decision on the grounds of unfair dismissal and was seeking the rest of his contract to be paid out. In the meantime, he would rehab at St George's Park, the FA's national facility at Burton-on-Trent.

The sacking soured the relationship between Keogh and Morris, who were always close. The defender felt badly let down by the club while the owner felt stung that the player would be part of such irresponsible actions.

Keogh eventually won his appeal and received compensation of around £2m. His road to recovery was ultimately successful and he has played for four clubs since his dismissal from Pride Park – Milton Keynes Dons, Huddersfield Town, Blackpool and Ipswich Town. However, the journey was dotted with draining and grim moments with his mental health suffering as a result.

'I wasn't feeling suicidal. I wasn't. Some days, I was in depression – I genuinely do believe that. But mainly I think I was right on the cusp of it. I was literally on the line for a lot of the time,' he told *The Guardian* on 1 October 2021.

Keogh also revealed a hidden factor at play during the same interview – he had lost his grandmother. Such an emotional blow threw his decision-making on the fateful evening.

'I would say I was a bit drunk,' Keogh says. 'I wasn't drinking heavily. I think with my nan passing, it was a combination of emotionally not being in a great place and having a few drinks. It's probably not a great combination for anyone.'

Keogh's reasoning for getting into Tom Lawrence's Range Rover that evening was routine. He saw Lawrence and a pair of passengers – who have never been revealed – in the car and Keogh had not spent the evening with Lawrence and therefore thought he was sober enough to drive.

'I hadn't spent the evening with Tom,' Keogh told *The Guardian*. 'I had no reason to believe he was over the limit. Everyone was in there before me so I didn't think, "Hang on a minute." It was just, "OK. I need to get home. Let's go." The next thing I know I'm waking up and speaking to the paramedics.'

Throughout it all, Keogh and Lawrence stayed in touch. Lawrence visited his old skipper, the pair would exchange text messages and speak on the phone. In an interview with Derby County's *Rampage Magazine* the following season, Lawrence would also address the issue – taking full responsibility for the accident.

Bennett was cagier when addressing the incident. Speaking with NewsAtDen in February 2020, after joining Millwall, he said he had spoken to Keogh without further elaboration, talked about he and Lawrence still being close friends and conceded he had 'messed up' and that he would still regret his decisions on that night when he's in his 60s and 70s but wished to move past the incident and focus on his playing career.

The repercussions bled into the seasons that followed. When Lawrence was named captain by manager Wayne Rooney ahead of 2021/22, the decision surprised several members of the Derby squad – partly because of the drink-driving incident – who felt there were better candidates, with Graeme Shinnie, Curtis Davies, Craig Forsyth and Colin Kazim-Richards all names brought up before Lawrence's.

4

Teething Problems

AN OPENING-DAY 2-1 victory away at Huddersfield Town was the perfect start for Phillip Cocu. Huddersfield had just been relegated from the Premier League and were pegged as one of the stronger teams in the Championship – so claiming a victory against them on their home soil instantly drew up a bigger groundswell of support for Derby's new manager. The Rams played at a slower yet more controlled pace that evening than fans had been used to seeing under Frank Lampard, but the early indication was that a less gung-ho approach could be what would make the team more consistent in the long run.

Cocu's football would be based around passing in tight spaces, timing, a high defensive line and positional switching with versatile players out of a 4-2-3-1 formation. In defending, Cocu would ask his players to condense the middle of the field and squeeze the opposition to the outside where the full-backs could deal with the threat – this also limited the chance to cut right down the middle of Derby and expose them in transition. There was much more to it than that – and as time went on it became more convoluted – but those were the core principles of it all.

Against Huddersfield, the team very much looked like a work in progress – taking an extra second to pass the ball here, a player out of position there. But overall there was enough to garner from the first performance of the season to expect much more from the team in the coming weeks and have Derby playing with Total Football methodology right at the heart of them.

That both goals, scored by Tom Lawrence, were of the highest quality – combining slick passing and movement with fizzing strikes and deft lobs – was a bonus. It had fans dreaming of football that a 1970s Ajax side would be proud of. The Dutch revolution was only just beginning.

A credible home 0-0 draw against Swansea City, who would eventually end up in the play-offs under the guidance of Steve Cooper, also garnered encouragement. But the worm ever so slowly started to turn as dominating possession-based performances were still not yielding results – and in some cases even goals were a struggle to come by.

In fact, Derby would not win another game until after the drink-driving accident, a run of seven winless (five draws, two defeats), when they had to rescue the points against Birmingham City at Pride Park. Rescue being the operative word as Derby had thrown away a 2-0 lead in the space of three second-half minutes and needed a Kelle Roos penalty save to keep them level before Jamie Paterson scored the winner.

Mixed in with the league frustrations was an upsetting 3-0 defeat to Nottingham Forest in the second round of the League Cup. Cocu made ten changes from the previous match, a 1-1 draw against West Bromwich Albion, and in the process handed debuts to Louie Sibley and Morgan Whittaker as well as giving some of the more fringe players at the time – Mason Bennett, Duane Holmes and Graeme Shinnie – minutes. The result, wholesale changes and performance received unpleasant reviews from the fans. Derby failed to even register a shot on target and were soundly beaten – the night capped off with a comedy goal involving Curtis Davies trying to clear the ball away, only for it to cannon off João Carvalho and into the back of Ben Hamer's net. The instant rapport Cocu had built up with the fans now lay at its lowest-ever point; that it happened so quickly was a concern, and that Cocu had, in many supporters' eyes, seemingly not understood the importance of the East Midlands derby had rapidly shortened any patience they were expected to have with him.

'I remember him after the game saying that he didn't care that much about the result or the performance as we were never going to win the cup anyway,' Holmes said. 'That, to me, said that he didn't understand the magnitude of the fixture. Doesn't matter whether it's in the Carabao [League] Cup, the league or a friendly – you want to win that game and the fans see that game as everything. I didn't understand at the time and I felt sorry for him because everything had been such a whirlwind in coming to the club, but that did him no favours early on.'

There was a dusting of sympathy to be had with the Dutchman, however. Cocu was still getting to grips with the squad he had inherited and arrived late to meet. He had barely had two months with them as a group and even less time with the new signings that were brought in. The League Cup games were always intended to be

TEETHING PROBLEMS

experimental fixtures – that the draw was so cruel as to hand Derby their fiercest rivals was not part of the plan. It was perhaps an early sign of the sort of scenario that would come to define Derby's seasons.

In the Championship, Derby had made a nasty habit of dropping points early in the season. Defensive softness, individual errors and missed chances of their own meant that after ten games they had let slip eight points from winning positions – easily the highest in the division. Derby would also enter an eight-game period where they would win one only to lose next time out, creating maddening frustration.

More damning would be the consistent away defeats. While their home record would become impressive as the season went on, Derby travelled poorly. After that opening-day away victory at Huddersfield they would not collect three points on the road again for six whole months – when they fought back from 2-1 down to beat Swansea City 3-2.

The manner of most of the losses would take their toll and the problem seemed to be deeply rooted. Derby would lose 3-0 on the road to Brentford, Fulham, Charlton Athletic and Reading while also losing 2-0 against Hull City and going 3-0 down against Bristol City before grabbing a couple of goals in a bid to claw back a draw – which they didn't manage. Cocu could be irritable with the media after such results. When one journalist asked if the manager should apologise to the fans after the 3-0 drubbing against Fulham – in which his team failed to register a single shot on target – he baulked:

'So you think it's a disgrace what we put on the pitch? I think we played a very strong team – the best team I've seen in this league. Sometimes you have to give credit to your opponent. Of course we can do better. But today we weren't capable of bringing extra to hurt Fulham. I'm always sad for the fans because they travel and it's a long journey.'

Part of Derby's problem was their passive nature away from home. So often playing with a high line but little press, teams found it easy to play over the top of them and get the defence on the back foot with little work. In fact, after the 2-2 away draw against Barnsley on 2 October, Derby would not pick up another away point, or score a single away goal, until Boxing Day against Wigan Athletic – a run of six matches.

After a 3-0 hammering against Brentford at the end of August, Cocu stormed into the press room shaking his head, took an uncomfortable seat on a plastic, almost school classroom-style chair and delivered a scathing assessment of his players:

'A lot [of work to be done]. I'm really surprised. That came out of nowhere how we played the first half. We knew it was a big game and we wanted to get a good result before the international break. I cannot accept our mentality and attitude. Compared to Brentford, it was such a big difference. Are you willing to give your maximum effort in offence and defence? And in the first 20 minutes there was such a big difference between my team and Brentford.

'It's not about how we concede the goals – it's about how we play the game. We cannot turn up here at 75 per cent of our best and just think we're going to play some nice football. Not in an away game. Not in a home game.

Not in any game. Never. I don't know where this attitude comes from.'

It was the sort of strong review which Cocu had refrained from handing out so far, but with live mics in front of him and sat high up in Griffin Park he let loose – much to the amazement of some of the squad.

'He never mentioned anything to any of the lads about a bad attitude,' Lowe recounted. 'He'd always just used to laugh it off and say it was the press making a big deal out of things or that he didn't say those things. But never once did he question our attitude behind closed doors.'

A little over a month later, after dropping two points in the dying embers at Barnsley, Cocu delivered a similar verdict about his team, questioning their desire to defend and their attitude.

It hurt some of the players, especially some of the more senior group who believed their manager should have kept such brutal criticisms behind closed doors. It was especially true considering that Cocu would never have conversations in private about the attitude of the players. He would often laugh off comments he made in the press when the squad saw them. Many, however, believed Cocu needed to put some of the dressing room on notice publicly and weed out some bad habits of the group.

While under Lampard the Rams played some champagne football, behind the scenes the dynamic could be difficult. Lampard never enjoyed confrontation, especially from senior players, and was more than willing to let certain issues slide to avoid getting into a row – Richard Keogh being one of the senior names Lampard elected to seldom push.

Some players expected more from Lampard in that sense – asking how someone who had played at the highest level, who'd had to manage egos in his own dressing rooms, which may include confrontation, and play under one of the most confrontational managers of all time in José Mourinho, could be so averse to conflict as a manager.

'I expected more from him as a man,' former Derby defender Andre Wisdom told *The Beautiful Game Podcast* in May 2023. 'I don't think he was honest to the team collectively. It was easy when everything was going well, but I think it was very cliquey. It felt like people spoke behind people's backs. We got battered by Aston Villa [4-0 in March 2019] and Lampard was screaming at me. I said some comments after the game and then Lampard just went in [on me]. But it had nothing to do with football really. It was more about me as a person, which was very strange to me. He said some things that were very strange. Very strange. He said I walked slowly, he said I bully people.'

While Cocu was not a man to scream and shout, he also created situations where conflict was a natural next step. He and striker Chris Martin got off to a tumultuous beginning to their relationship. Martin was a player who had strong opinions within the group and under previous management was allowed to air them often – usually unchallenged. That would change under Cocu and the pair bristled against each other for a while, so much so that Martin leaving during the summer window was very much on the cards. Martin had been attracting interest from a couple of Championship clubs but it was League One and Scotland where most of the suitors lay. Martin was content to stay at Pride Park and fight for his place, although Cocu originally did not envision him getting many minutes. In fact it was only when Martin came off the bench to score the goal which snatched a 1-1 draw against Leeds United that Cocu finally had to relent and accept him as his best centre-forward option.

'It baffled me that Chris couldn't get a game,' Max Lowe remembered. 'Cocu was so wedded to this 4-3-3 and said that Martin didn't fit what he wanted to do. But from my standpoint – and a lot of lads' standpoint, too – Chris was exactly what the system needed to work. He'd have never got a game I don't think unless he scored that goal against Leeds.'

That Cocu would be on record several times towards the end of the season making it very clear he would like Martin, who was out of contract, to stay spoke volumes of the pair's ability to meet in the middle. However, it also documented Cocu's reliance on Martin as a player and perhaps his shortsightedness at not believing the burly striker was good enough to suit his system.

Martin's style of play was both robust and deft. He could hold the ball up without too many issues and play in his runners from central or out wide. He also possessed the deft touch capabilities to flick clever balls around the corner to those rushing beyond him without having to break stride. Martin could also work the channels and pressure opposition full-backs. He could often be spotted dropping so far deep he would be an extra midfielder and allow for the positional switching Cocu so wanted to favour. All of that, plus his goal threat, made him tailor-made for Cocu and his system. That the Dutchman failed to realise that until eight games into the season was an oversight – and this early uncertainty in their relationship played a small part in Martin leaving for pastures new at the end of the season even with Cocu eventually campaigning for him to stay. Martin wanted assurances of his usage as well as a decent contract – and the trust was not all the way back. While Martin's importance to the team grew as the season went on, he would only finish 90 minutes 11 times all campaign. Cocu recognised his importance but it was obvious the Dutchman also wanted another option, preferably in front of Martin, and that was where some of the mistrust between the two lay.

Some even believed that Cocu was only publicly saying he wanted to keep Martin as he knew it was the smart PR play for the fans. But the Dutchman was smart. He understood what fans wanted to hear and he himself was trying to garner all the support he could, especially as the campaign was not playing out as everybody wanted – Derby were less play-off contenders than they were a middling outfit struggling for any semblance of consistency or identity.

Another player quickly unsure of his new boss was Lowe. The left-back had recently come back from a loan spell at Aberdeen and was attracting interest from Rangers and Brentford. Having spent the lion's share of his Derby career to that point either in the academy or loaned out, Lowe was interested in exploring his options considering he saw Scott Malone ahead of him in the pecking order once again. But Cocu was unwilling to let the left-back go.

'It was deadline day and I remember my agent telling me that Brentford had made a bid for me and it had been rejected. I wasn't aware they were interested in me, and at the time I was behind Scott [Malone] at left-back, currently playing out of position at right-back and it was a bit frustrating. I wanted to discuss things with Phillip.

'I asked why the bid got rejected and he looked at me and said they hadn't bid for me – but then on the TV in his office, Sky Sports flashed up and they announced "Brentford have bid for Max Lowe turned down" and I pointed to it. He just laughed and said I need to crack on. I didn't like that, I felt he wasn't being honest with me.'

Lowe was one of the more featured players of Cocu's tenure, finishing 90 minutes 21 times – though seven of those came when he was deployed at right-back to cover for the injured Jayden Bogle. But a large source of frustration came from Cocu's inability to play the same left-back week after week. Lowe, Malone and Craig Forsyth all rotated at the position, to the annoyance of them and the rest of the defence who were trying to build up some kind of chemistry and cohesion for the season ahead. Many pointed to the constant changing of the back line as a main reason why Derby only kept nine clean sheets all season.

Another player who was in limbo to start Cocu's tenure was Curtis Davies. The defender was coming off a torn Achilles which he suffered in November 2018 and found himself behind Richard Keogh and new loan signing Matt Clarke in the pecking order. Davies was an old-school defender and not perhaps fitting with what Cocu wanted in his team. Keogh – as evidenced by his progressive run and passing during the second leg of the 2019 play-off semi-final victory over Leeds – was not afraid to carry the ball, make passes and even run into midfield. Clarke could also be relied upon to step up the pitch while Derby attempted to create an overload elsewhere with one of their midfielders. Davies, largely, was none of that. He would put his head in where it hurt, he would throw his body in front of balls and, if in doubt, clear it out. Nothing fancy, but highly effective. Davies could also be counted upon to be a vocal leader and a calming presence – but none of it really buzzed Cocu. That Davies was still around was more a result of circumstance rather than Cocu realising his worth.

Davies said, 'It was a simple case of him signing Matt Clarke and I was still recovering from my injury. But I was fit. I was doing the pre-season and stuff like that. But he didn't want to take a look at me. We played the pre-season game against Bristol City and I played 20 minutes but then after that I was always in the second-string side. And I would be playing with the kids – I probably had more starts than them boys put together. It was hard for me mentally because I'm trying to get myself back going, and I'm judging myself mentally as to where my game is after seven months out, but I'm with the kids.

'When the season started I was in the squad against Huddersfield and Swansea, but then I was the 19th man against Stoke. I went in on Monday and told him that I didn't have any issues not being in the squad, but if that is the case then leave me at home. I don't want to be a negative influence – not with words but perhaps my body language – on the boys about not being in the squad. He apologised and we went on from that.

'But I didn't have a future at the club. I remember the night after the team-bonding session that all went wrong, the manager had told me that at the last minute I could go. But it was last minute – I couldn't get anything over here. I'd been out for seven months, the window was closing. I was up at 2am looking for countries where the transfer window was still open – Qatar, UAE, Australia.'

Cocu had offered Davies a chance to get some minutes in his legs in the under-23s. But upon discovering the academy game was on a Sunday, Davies realised that he would be omitted from both senior squads for Saturday and the following Tuesday. That realisation irritated Davies, who believed his new manager was trying to force him out of the club for good.

That rule, however, was not so universal. If players had one criticism of their new manager, it was his unwillingness to criticise individuals if they had made mistakes.

'He was very much about the team first. Even if one of the boys made a mistake and it cost us a goal, which then cost us points, it would still be about the team in the dressing room,' explained Lowe. 'Sometimes you just wanted him to dig somebody out, hold one of us accountable and then it makes you realise that there's no hiding place. It's easy to keep making mistakes and not being accountable if all the time you can just hide behind "oh, but it's all part of the team".'

One dressing room source said, 'He was a really nice man and I think he struggled to hold certain people accountable for fear of upsetting them personally, but also he wanted everybody to buy into the team and not have any egos – which is hard when you're dealing with lads who have just come off a play-off final appearance, had done things a certain way and had a certain culture already installed. I think when Wayne [Rooney] came in, it made things a bit worse for him. Wayne would have some shocking performances at times, but it was always about the team. Team this, team that. And then even Wayne would have a scream and shout at some of the lads – even if he was rubbish – and it just started to create a weird dynamic between some of the lads.'

There was also a concern that Cocu's Derby were soft – a team that would roll over at the first sign of adversity on the pitch, or would be more focused on playing neat football and could not mix it up in what can often be a rough-and-tumble Championship season. Derby only took 13 points from games in which they fell behind, and recorded 16 losses in matches in which they faced a one-goal deficit. The team was not hardy by any stretch of the imagination, and in a bid to show some steel they racked up a remarkable ill-disciplined performance during a 3-0 defeat away at Reading in December.

The scoreline was strange in that Derby could conceivably have taken a positive result from the game, which would have been special considering Scott Malone was sent off after three minutes and conceded a penalty, which the hosts scored. The Rams had responded to the early double setback with a flurry of attacking intent and, had Tom Lawrence's effort snuck the other side of the post immediately after Reading went 1-0 up, the match could have gone down a very different path. Yet, instead, it was the same old result – another hammering away from home.

More notable, however, was the eight yellow cards – plus the red – that the Rams collected. Derby lost their heads in the second half, picking up seven of their eight yellows, and the frustrations boiled over as yet another away match got out of hand, and this one put them on the back foot so quickly causing an extra layer of disappointment. Though not ideal, Cocu chose to put a positive spin on the ill-discipline:

'I saw it in a positive way because it means that we react together as a team. I think there were some moments where there were some provocations from the opponent after they went 2-0 up. They have some tricks and play in front of the ref. It's their game. But we show what we stand for and you don't mess with us. Sometimes you have to stand up and get a booking, you just have to make sure it's worth it.'

It was a message Cocu wanted to send out of unity, of his side going down swinging and not being taken for mugs – but that it came off the back of yet another disappointing, long away day left many fans feeling irritated and not receptive to hearing that their team losing their cool when faced with adversity was a positive sign. It didn't help that Derby were languishing in 17th – and would soon slip to 18th, their lowest position of the season, five days later when they needed a last-gasp Martyn Waghorn goal to snatch a point at Wigan Athletic on a drizzly Boxing Day.

Like many managers, Cocu would also use the media to send out a message if and when he needed to – be that taking aim at a player, the board or, on occasion, the officials. That he was usually so well measured and soft-spoken made his public criticisms sting more. The first glimpse of Cocu taking aim at a player directly came after a 1-1 home draw against Huddersfield in February 2020. Frustrations had been bubbling up after yet another away defeat in which Derby conceded three goals, this time against Bristol City three days earlier. It threatened to be another embarrassment on the road until Waghorn and Martin pulled two goals back to set up a grandstand finish. But Derby still lost 3-2.

For the Huddersfield game, both Bogle and Lowe were dropped – chief offenders at Ashton Gate for subpar defending. Andre Wisdom also had a poor showing but was perhaps the best of a bad bunch on that night. Bogle was brought on as a substitute for Wisdom with just 11 minutes remaining against the Terriers and with Derby holding a precious 1-0 lead. Within two minutes of his introduction he had sent a poor defensive header into the path of Harry Toffolo. To compound the mistake, the young right-back showed his opposite number inside, instead of towards the touchline and Toffolo was then screaming down on the Derby goal. He smashed a low shot into the far corner and it was 1-1. After the game Cocu raged publicly at Bogle, questioning his attitude and even whether one of the stars of the previous campaign could do the basics of defending.

'It's bad defending. It's never just one mistake, there are a few. But it starts with the clearance with the header … Bogle. He gives it away so easily with no pressure on him. Then he doesn't push him [Toffolo] to the outside, instead shows him inside – it's basics,' Cocu said with a clenched jaw. 'For me it confirmed he was upset that he didn't play. But you have to put your ego aside and when your team-mates need you, you need to be 100 per cent in the game. It was not good enough from his side. I don't think confidence is a problem – he's a confident player. He has a lot of potential going forward. But he has to learn that as a defender, you have a big responsibility to defend. You have to switch on, be aggressive and be prepared to match the tempo of the game.'

The criticism was also a hidden message to the rest of the squad as Cocu was clearly still irked at the lapses costing points just three days after a defensive disaster cost Derby all three, but Bogle was the lightning rod for the criticism and it was not well received. Bogle discovered his manager's displeasure of his performance online when the comments started to circulate. A couple of players who were close to Bogle called him to discuss what Cocu had said, and why he had chosen to do it publicly.

'Jayden was upset,' Lowe said. 'And I could understand why. All season it was about team responsibility and then he goes and absolutely throws you under the bus like that. It was his mistake, and there's no arguing that. But if you're going to consistently talk about team mistakes and everything about the team, you're going to be a bit taken aback when the gaffer publicly does that to you.'

There was further fallout to come. On the post-match episode of *Sportscene* on BBC Radio Derby, former Derby County midfielder and co-commentator Craig Ramage was giving his assessment of the draw and performance in general when he said, 'When I look at certain players, their body language, their stance, the way they act, you just feel, hold on a minute, he needs pulling down a peg or two.

'So I'd probably say that about all the young black lads, all the young advice if they wanted it, that, you know, it's about, when you are struggling for form, you are going through a sticky patch, it's about going back to basics, working hard, and doing the right things.'

The soundbite went viral, garnered national news coverage and immediately sent the local reaction into overdrive. How could this remark be made? How was it allowed to slip through editing? Why did the BBC upload it, before then trying to sneakily remove it and hope nobody would notice?

The very next day the BBC terminated its relationship with Ramage, stating, 'These were entirely unacceptable comments and we will no longer be working with Craig.'

An investigation was immediately launched and was treated with such severity that Chris Burns, the head of audio and digital at BBC England, got involved and went to the station to probe further. Presenter Chris Coles was also temporarily suspended from his duties and left in the dark as to whether he would have a job to go back to once it was over.

Coles was anxious and expressed remorse privately for not fully taking on board what Ramage was saying. Coles was often a one-man band when it came to production, conducting interviews, teeing up next segments and scrolling through a company iPad to stay on task. During Ramage's tirade, Coles had been manning said tablet, fiddling with audio tuners and, generally, not really listening to his colleague when he let out a disinterested 'hmm' as Ramage continued. This at the time seemed to many like a sign of agreement with his co-host but was later determined to be Coles simply not really listening with his eyes and hands on several other things but wanting to convey that he was paying attention. There was also intense scrutiny aimed at the editing team who let the comment go unedited in their original version before it was hastily taken out of the audio and re-uploaded, with the feeling that some at the BBC attempted to brush the comments under the carpet.

After nine days, the investigation was concluded with the BBC stating, 'These comments were entirely unacceptable and we have already said we won't be working with Craig any more. Following a thorough investigation, we are confident this won't happen again. We would like to apologise to Derby County and particularly the players for the distress caused by these comments.'

Coles was able to return to his job, much to his and every Derby fan's delight. Players did not even hold Coles accountable with the presenter able to return to Moor Farm and interview players.

'You do things like that all the time, don't you?' Lowe said in reference to Coles making unengaging noises as Ramage spoke. 'Like you're not really listening but you just make a noise to make it feel like the other person isn't just talking into space or whatever. I'm not mad at him anyway – he never said anything racist. So why would I be mad at him?'

Ramage issued a 'heartfelt apology' in which he said the error was 'unintentional' and 'in no way reflects my personal views'. Despite his public statement, however, he never contacted either Lowe or Bogle to personally apologise.

'I never heard from him,' Lowe remarked. 'I remember talking to Jayden about it a couple of weeks after – he never heard from Craig either. He apologised on Twitter, but he couldn't call us personally to apologise.'

Lowe took to Instagram in the immediate aftermath of the incident to post a statement which read, 'Racial ignorance, stereotyping and intolerance negatively affects the image of impressionable young footballers and creates an unnecessary divide in society. As a professional footballer at an ambitious, high-profile Championship club I know that my performances will be scrutinised and I have no problem with that whatsoever – but I do not think it is acceptable for myself and my team-mate Jayden Bogle to be judged by the colour of our skin.'

'At first I regretted posting about it on my Instagram, but then I didn't,' Lowe said. 'I was the oldest out of me and Jayden, I wanted to show a bit of leadership. I didn't consult with the club or my agent. I just decided I was going to do it. I remember actually listening to that episode of *Sportscene* in the car on the way home. I've always listened to BBC Derby after games and even when I was a kid my dad would have it on. Then somebody sent me the clip and I had to rewind it about four or five times to check what I was hearing was right.

'I didn't even play in that game – so why has he come for me? It felt like a spillover from the Bristol City game. I didn't understand it. But then after I'd posted and said something about it I didn't expect some of our own fans to shout things at me. I'd be warming up and people would shout "GRASS" or reference the clip, "YOU NEED PULLING DOWN A PEG". But I understood it to a degree. Craig had been around the club for a long time, fans of a certain era remember him fondly and all that – but to support him after he went on air and said what he said was mad to me.'

The performance from Bogle against Huddersfield and the post-game comments by Cocu marked the beginning of the end for their relationship. While Bogle would continue to play a key role in the squad, it was clear that Cocu did not believe he had the tools to defend, nor the temperament to learn how to defend. Conversely, Bogle went from being a favourite under Frank Lampard to a challenging second season as a first-team player and found the peaks and troughs which came with taking the next step in development, as well as adapting to a new manager and new methods.

Lampard never played with the handbrake on – sometimes to the point of recklessness. But the attack-minded nature of his teams allowed Bogle to flourish to the tune of ten Championship assists in 2018/19 and a whole host of swashbuckling dribbles and runs into the opposition half with little thought of defensive duties. Cocu demanded safety first. Suddenly the traits which put Bogle at the top of exciting players to watch were being curtailed. But Cocu did have a point – Bogle was still learning his trade at right-back. As a converted winger, attacking came very naturally to him. But defending was more of a challenge. With Cocu unwilling to shift to a formation which would offer Bogle protection – such as making him a wing-back in a 3-4-3 or 5-3-2 – the academy graduate had to learn the hard way and thus the more defensively minded Andre Wisdom was higher up the pecking order for Cocu.

Cocu had grown frustrated with the slow progress of the team, and said as much in December 2019 ahead of a vital January window which would see Rooney join and, what Cocu hoped, would be a chance to further add to the squad in what would truly be his first chance to recruit players after the hodge-podge signings over the summer which he largely did not have chance to properly oversee.

'There is always something you hope for when you come to developing a team – the young players, the chemistry in the team – you want them to put it together,' Cocu said. 'We had a little bit too much to deal with [off the pitch] to make that happen. It's not an excuse, but it is a reason why it's going slower than we had in mind. We have to keep developing the team and in the winter break we have to keep developing some important parts of the team and signings will be important to some of the things we want to build. But we had hoped we'd be further along when we started working here.'

The job was not just about getting in the right personnel and shipping out those who did not fit the Dutchman's ideology both on the field and off it, however. One of the things Cocu did look to stamp out, and even more so after the drink-driving accident, was drinking.

Derby had famously run up a £2,800 bar bill in the wake of defeating Leeds in the second leg of the play-off semi-final in 2019 to send them to Wembley. The tab included 209 beers, 75 Jägermeisters, 65 shots of Grey Goose and 54 shots of Sambuca. The bill did not just represent the players, however, but also backroom staff and even some of the club communications and media staff, and was in part evidence of the great camaraderie that Lampard and his assistant Jody Morris had built with people beyond just the players.

After the September 2019 drink-driving incident, the club did not organise a Christmas party for fear of a backlash, given what had gone on. Instead a Christmas lunch was organised, which was usually reserved for staff only, for all players from the various age groups and women's team as Derby looked to strengthen their One Club identity even further by having everyone mixing. It was a decision which was taken after a meeting between Cocu, Morris and the staff at the club. Derby County Ladies FC did also throw their Christmas party, too, even tweeting out how successful it was.

Cocu was the opposite of Lampard in nearly every way. The Dutchman seldom drank, only occasionally enjoying a glass of red wine with dinner – a custom he had been introduced to while playing for Barcelona. While Lampard was energetic on the touchline and more interactive with the fans, Cocu cut a much more stoic figure in the dugout and rarely emoted more than a casual wave of the arm to the stands, an exasperated throw back of his head or a simple fist pump after a goal. It prompted accusations that he was not a passionate man. Cocu was not cold by any stretch of the imagination, but he would keep his distance and instilled a manager and employee relationship which was much more cut and dry than under Lampard. The lines that seemed slightly blurred under Lampard were more harshly drawn under Cocu.

5

The Youth Movement

PART OF Mel Morris's vision for Derby heading into the future was having a vibrant squad full of youth; by the time the 2021/22 season rolled around, he had wanted half of the 25-man squad to consist of academy graduates. Under Frank Lampard, just four players bred in the academy made appearances – Max Bird, Jayden Bogle, Max Lowe and Mason Bennett – in what was very much a 'win now' season for the Rams. The signings of Ashley Cole and Efe Ambrose further blocked the paths of academy talent. One in particular was bittersweet about the arrival of Cole. Max Lowe had spent most of his time as an understudy or out on loan and had started the season with Aberdeen before returning in January and logging 90 minutes in a 2-0 defeat to Leeds United. Then Cole arrived and Lowe was promptly sent back out on loan to Aberdeen once more.

'When Ashley came in, I was buzzing,' Lowe said in an interview with The Athletic. 'He's the best left-back to play in my generation. When I moved to left-back all I did was watch Ashley. I remember we had a chat in the physio room before I went out on loan and he told me not to be disappointed, to come back and knuckle down. He said he'd heard good things about me.

'Me being a young lad … I wasn't really having it. I was disappointed. I wanted to stay. And I told him that straight up. He laughed and we went separate ways. When I was at Aberdeen he'd text me. He was watching some of my games and giving me feedback. He was really good. He understood how much I looked up to him, so anything he said I took in. But I was still annoyed that I had to go back out on loan.'

It was the success of Jayden Bogle, who was one of the stars under Lampard's Derby, scoring two goals and logging ten assists, a converted winger-turned-full-back bursting with speed, attacking initiative and an often deadly final ball, which prompted Morris to believe that, if given the correct opportunities under Phillip Cocu, the next wave of young talent could thrive.

Bogle had been plucked from Swindon's academy in 2016 and would play two seasons for Derby's youth team before being promoted into the senior setup. He was electric down the wing, a player capable of great skill and speed, able to beat his man time and time again and deliver a deadly ball, tailor-made for Lampard's style of football – swashbuckling with little regard for defensive nous and an inability to defend the transition. However, it was those areas where Bogle needed the greatest refinement. But those were skills to be developed at a later date. His rise, and the subsequent interest in him, made Morris eager to capitalise on his current crop.

Bogle had drawn interest from Burnley but, more interestingly, AC Milan had cast an eye over Derby's young right-back. Milan internally were undergoing a new model of buying up young, ascending Championship stars and then selling them back to English clubs at an inflated price – Nottingham Forest's Matty Cash was also someone the Italian giants were keen on. However, Milan were reluctant to pay anything more than £8m for Bogle, who at the time Derby rated at north of £10m.

It seemed an ideal time to capitalise on such an idea. By the end of the 2018/19 season Derby had just won the U18 Premier League for the first time in their history, blasting away a much-fancied Arsenal side to win 5-2 – including a hat-trick from Archie Brown. The triumph netted the young Rams further opportunities in the shape of a first campaign in the UEFA Youth League in which they would have the chance to test themselves against some of the best youth sides across Europe.

Of the squad named against Arsenal, six went on to make first-team appearances for the Rams (Jordan Brown, Eiran Cashin, Lee Buchanan, Morgan Whittaker, Louie Sibley and Jason Knight) – while Max Bird, who played the full 90 minutes against the Gunners, had been blooded with the senior squad in the 2018/19 season, making eight appearances under Lampard.

Most of the players introduced to the first team were a success. Knight, an unused substitute in the 2019 play-off semi-final second leg at Leeds and also at Wembley against Aston Villa, made his first senior appearance in the 2-1 away victory over Huddersfield Town to open up 2019/20 and proved to be one of Derby's most valuable players that season, playing in multiple roles and scoring six goals – including a brace on 30 December to beat

Charlton Athletic in a game in which the Rams had to play 73 minutes with ten men following Krystian Bielik's straight red card. Knight would operate primarily in central midfield but would also be known to play on either wing if Cocu required extra cover on the flanks. The trade-off was that Knight rarely had the breakaway speed to execute fast counterattacks, but his willingness to run, work hard and seemingly never tire made him invaluable. He was even compared to his fellow countryman Roy Keane by some Derby coaching staff who saw shades of the tenacious former Manchester United midfielder in his game. So ferocious could Knight be that once during training he went straight through a wooden panel by a pitch when trying to close down his man and win the ball.

Knight was scrappy, and although he was not world-class at any one technical ability, he was very good at nearly everything. One area where he could be depended on was his work rate. Knight would cover every blade of grass, in any position he was asked to play, and do a solid job. His performances garnered the attention of his soon-to-be team-mate and manager, too. During a late December fixture, just days away from when Wayne Rooney could officially be registered as a Derby player, he joined RamsTV as a pundit and showered the young Irishman with praise:

'I've been really impressed with the way they've trained, particularly Knighty. His energy, his attitude. He almost reminds me of myself when I was younger in terms of no fear.

'And he's got an aggression about him, not in terms of how he's tackling, but in terms of how he runs, how he gets about the pitch. I'm looking forward to seeing how they do as I feel he can give us a lot of energy and a lot of creativity.'

Some argued such flexibility and willingness hurt Knight's chances of playing in his most desired position – centrally, as a number eight. But nevertheless he refused to complain and continued on doing a job regardless. His star began to rise so much that eventually Premier League clubs began to test Derby's resistance to keep hold of one of their top young stars – Burnley, the top suitors, had made several inquiries as to his availability in January 2020 and resurrected their interest in January 2022 but at each and every turn they were rebuked. So strong was the club's desire to keep hold of the Ireland international in the winter of 2022 that Rooney, in the managerial position at this point, declared that 'as long as I'm here Jason Knight will not be leaving this football club' and he was true to his word.

Louie Sibley had to wait a little longer for his opportunity to shine. The blond dynamo was rocketing to notoriety within Derby's ranks. An eight-goal, three-assist youth-team season in 2018/19 put him on the map. And he would soon follow up with five goals and seven assists in just half a season in 2019/20 – the reason his time was limited there was due to his exposure to the first-team squad. The talented forward continued to shine in the youth setup to begin 2019/20, and logged four assists and a goal in four UEFA Youth League appearances, but had found his first-team opportunities limited to a start in the League Cup defeat at Nottingham Forest and 20 minutes from the bench in the 3-0 Championship loss at Reading. But that all changed in early March, less than a week before football would stop for three months due to the Covid-19 pandemic. Sibley was given the nod at home against Blackburn Rovers and scored a thunderbolt from nearly 30 yards. Although he had to wait over three months for his next start, he picked up where he left off with a hat-trick against Millwall in a 3-2 victory as Derby mounted a late play-off charge behind closed doors. Such was Sibley's rise to prominence that Cocu remarked that 'nobody could afford' him when teams started sniffing around – including Leeds United.

One of Sibley's downfalls was his tendency to play on the edge, annoying opponents, backchatting with referees and getting into frequent shoving matches of varied temperatures.

'Sometimes I need to just have a word in his ear – doesn't surprise me that he gets into it to be honest,' Max Bird said in a June 2020 interview with The Athletic. 'It's part of what makes his game so good though is that intensity. You don't want him to lose it. You just need a calm voice in his ear every now and again, that's all.'

'They call him the firestarter,' Sibley's dad, Andy, told The Athletic in March 2020. 'He's got a spark and he just goes. He can get everybody going.'

Some players believed that coaches encouraged some of Sibley's worse habits on the training ground – actively egging him on to kick at the ankles of his team-mates in training in a battle to get the ball. It could, and often would, frustrate more senior players. But others saw nothing wrong with a little competitive fire – especially in periods when Derby had to show fight on the pitch to keep their heads above water.

Despite the early heroics of his senior career, Sibley was still a young player finding his feet. His form was wildly inconsistent following his breakthrough couple of months at the back end of 2019/20. In fact, after his Millwall hat-trick during Project Restart, Sibley would only score one goal, on the final day of the season, in his next 30 senior appearances before breaking his drought with a dramatic equaliser in a 2-2 home draw against Brentford at Pride Park in March 2021. When Wayne Rooney was installed as manager following Cocu's sacking, he demanded more from Sibley. Sibley had hit the bar in the dying embers of a 1-0 defeat to Millwall at Pride Park on 13 March 2021 when Derby were battling to keep their Championship status. The effort seemed to leave his manager unimpressed.

'He needs to do more, he has to do more when he comes on,' Rooney outlined. 'He has come on in a few games and he needs to show me that he deserves to play because I know he is an exciting player, he can score goals, he can create goals.

'I am not having a go at Louie Sibley, he is a fantastic player and a fantastic talent but it shows what I think of him that I know he can do better. For me he has to do better to start.'

As for Max Bird, he had already been blooded under Lampard but cemented his place in the side under Cocu and remained a regular under Rooney, then Liam Rosenior and latterly Paul Warne. Such was Bird's importance to the side after his emergence that ahead of the 2022/23 season he was named as vice-captain of the club.

Bird rose to prominence as a technically gifted central midfielder who was drawing comparisons to Michael

Carrick. Not long after his father passed in February 2019, Bird sped off from the hospital to play for Derby's under-23s, showing a determination that has typified his career to date with his progress being anything but linear. He got his first action under Cocu in a League Cup first-round tie against Scunthorpe United but was substituted off at half-time and it impacted his confidence. Bird himself knew that his 45 minutes had not been his finest hour, but he hardly expected to be hooked for the performance. And seeing his peers get exposure in the first team while he spent some time back with the academy hurt his belief. Nevertheless, he did press on before making another breakthrough in the senior team just before Christmas. When Rooney joined in January, he was full of praise for Bird. In fact Rooney was almost glued to his central midfield partner both on and off the pitch. Bird was learning lessons in real time with his childhood hero and was determined to make Rooney's praise stick.

Rooney, during his time with Derby, remained constantly baffled that Bird was never selected for an England under-21 squad, but even the former Manchester United superstar had to enact some tough love on the midfielder. Entering January 2021, Bird was having a poor season – as were the rest of the squad, which led to their position in the relegation zone – and Rooney, now in sole managerial charge, sat his player down for a meeting in a bid to get Bird back on the right track.

'We sat down with Max last January I think it was and told him he wouldn't play many games,' Rooney said in a press conference in January 2022. 'We knew he would be frustrated with that but there were things we wanted him to improve on, which we worked with him on and really we were getting ready for the season, and it has shown he worked extremely hard. He got his head down and tried to improve himself, he did that and he's a vital player for us and he has played every game.'

But for every success of the academy, there were some who fell away from the glory they were promised for one reason or another.

Curiously, Archie Brown, the hat-trick hero of that U18 Premier League Final against Arsenal, never made his way into the first-team squad. Brown started life as a centre-back and at 17 years old he was already 6ft 2in and as wide as a fridge, often battering his opposition with his bullish style. But Brown also possessed excellent speed, electric acceleration and ballerina-like feet. Those gifts meant that he was soon repurposed as a left-winger but could also be used in a full-back role. Cocu was a fan of Brown's and invited the young match-winner to train with the first team once a week to get used to the standard of senior football. However, there were a few red flags against Brown which some of the coaching staff sought to put a stop to. First was his consistency. Some members of the backroom team felt it wasn't enough for Brown to turn in dominating performances when he was 'in the mood' and be so lacklustre when he wasn't. Although Brown made headlines with his treble against the Gunners, he was seen very much as a boom-or-bust prospect with very little in between. If he was ever going to make waves in the first team, he needed to be more consistent. Some even believed that his performance against Arsenal left Brown feeling 'over-confident' in himself and that his form suffered as a result. However, consistency was hard to come by for the youngster when, by the time his Derby career ended in June 2021, he had played in four different positions – left-wing, left wing-back, left-back and centre-back.

Another issue was his tendency to get frustrated if things didn't go his way in a match. If his opposition defender had Brown's number when it came to one-on-one battles, then his head would go down, or he would attempt elaborate dribbles to make up for the previous mistake. Finally there were distractions. His subsequent move to Switzerland – with Lausanne Sport – was in part to remove Brown from distractions and bad groups closer to home. A player seemingly with the world at his feet could easily see his career derailed if he fell in with a bad crowd. There was also the issue of playing time. Brown was offered a fresh deal at the end of the 2020/21 season but declined the terms in part because he saw his pathway to first-team football blocked by the likes of Craig Forsyth, Lee Buchanan, Tom Lawrence, Kamil Jóźwiak and others.

Striker Jahmal Hector-Ingram was cast off by West Ham United and, determined to find a club where he could break into the first team, joined Derby knowing he would go straight into the academy setup. Hector-Ingram then scored ten goals in 17 appearances for Derby's under-23s in the 2019/20 season before the three-month hiatus. Cocu had plans to bring him into the senior setup following the resumption of football, but there was just one problem – Hector-Ingram showed back up to training in June not up to the required fitness standards of the Dutch coach, although he did go on to make a handful of substitute appearances. There were other issues, too, even at academy level where he was so prolific. Coaches wanted Hector-Ingram to work harder off the ball, track back and make better runs in behind instead of being a typical poacher inside the opposition penalty area. Hector-Ingram got limited chances in the senior side, featuring in eight games, all from the bench, and totalling just 65 minutes – his final appearance for Derby being a one-minute cameo in a 1-0 victory over Bristol City in January 2021.

From one potentially exciting attacker to another, Tyree Wilson also failed to live up to the heights many had set for him. He had endured a horrendous stabbing incident in July 2020 and suffered serious injuries, sustaining them to his nose, collarbone and near his heart, and he was lucky to not be killed. His attacker, Andrew Marshall, who stabbed Wilson with an eight-inch knife, was jailed for more than six years for carrying out the attack. While Wilson worked on his physical rehab, his mental health took a toll. Derby supported him while he rehabbed and offered him support for his mental health also, but Wilson was never quite the same player again.

Wilson was once again in a place to play football during the 2021/22 season but in a bid to keep him away from distractions some around him felt it beneficial if he moved clubs – even abroad. Wilson lived in the St Ann's area of Nottingham. It was an area where Wilson, and those around him, could get into trouble easily and as a result he needed to be away. Wilson was offered a trial at Brentford in April 2022 but only on the condition that Derby released him, which it is believed they refused to do as the club were still weighing up their retained list.

The club continued to produce talent aside from their U18 Premier League-winning season, until they were made to ship them off to stay afloat. Dylan Williams was used as a left-back by Rooney at times during the early months of the 2021/22 season, still aged only 16, and the manager would often single out his young starlet for praise. It was partly true, but also partly a ploy to try and keep the youngsters at the club as other suitors sniffed around. Rooney was trying to convince players there was a pathway to the first team at Pride Park – which there was based on track record, but also there were opportunities due to the lack of senior players. He managed to convince some to stay. Williams, however, was sold to Chelsea in January 2022. All of this of course was not of Rooney's own volition. Derby's manager fought strongly to keep his most prized young assets for the sake of the season in hand, but also for future planning. But the club had been in administration for four months by the time of Williams's departure and the sale of Derby's brightest young prospects was required to keep cash flow coming into the club.

Another player ushered away by a Premier League club was exciting attacking midfielder Kaide Gordon. Those in the Derby academy setup raved about the slight, nimble youngster and believed he would be 'something special'. Rooney would include Gordon in matchday squads – giving him his debut as a 16-year-old as a substitute at Birmingham City in December 2020 – again to offer an olive branch to the first team. However, the secret was soon getting out – Manchester United were also interested in taking Gordon's talents to the north-west – and it became almost impossible to keep hold of him.

Staff around Moor Farm praised Gordon as 'the best 16-year-old in the country'. His development was no surprise as he had rocketed through age groups at Moor Farm since he was nine years old and by the time he was 14, he was already being selected for under-16s football – he was a full year ahead of most of his peers. Derby eventually got around £2m for him in compensation from Liverpool in February 2021 with a 20 per cent sell-on clause for the future – the club were trying to future-proof in case Gordon later moved for £50m and a large windfall could come their way. However, due to the financial difficulties Derby would later run into, the two clubs would settle on a one-time payment to make the clause null, which underlined just how strapped for cash the Rams were.

As the finances started to dry up, so did the talent in the academy and Derby were left to pick up players released from other academies – which did bring some joy. Louie Watson was released by West Ham and provided Derby with a small spark upon his arrival in the summer of 2020 but it was never enough. In came cast-offs from Manchester United, Arsenal, West Ham, Aston Villa and more. The clubs the players had been let go from were, of course, those of the elite – but the players were also struggling to find takers elsewhere around the football pyramid and Derby pounced, needing warm bodies through the door as it were.

Rooney also recognised the club was in a tough position and also bristled at the fact that young players, such as Omari Kellyman, a 16-year-old Northern Ireland international who signed with Aston Villa, had been picked off seemingly without his knowledge.

'I lost a player this morning, a 16-year-old local lad. I got a text message from the club secretary this morning that a deal had been agreed with Aston Villa,' Rooney said the day after a 2-0 defeat to Huddersfield in February 2022. 'He's a local lad from Derby, he didn't want to leave the club. I had him and his parents in the office. They were so proud he was on the bench. He wanted to play for Derby County. When you see young local lads getting sold from the football club, it's hard.

'It's a tough one for me and the staff to take. I am not from Derby, but I know what it is like to come through an academy and have those dreams of playing for your team. It is a tough one for me and the staff to take.'

Derby were not only losing senior players, they were starting to relinquish many of the young stars Morris had poured so much money into the club to create. It was a turn of events that deeply hurt the owner but was necessary for the survival of the club.

6

The Charge

AS DERBY fans grew impatient at the lack of movement in the January 2020 transfer window, and Phillip Cocu constantly called for reinforcements to be added – also saying that Rooney's signing was not enough, after the 1-1 Boxing Day draw at Wigan Athletic – behind the scenes things were starting to fall apart, which explained the lack of new signings.

Cocu had complained about the need for fresh blood in the group, and the club had made a push to sign Leicester City centre-back Filip Benković – a move which would have seen Curtis Davies once more surplus to requirements. Cocu also wanted to add an extra striker, as Rooney was being deployed in midfield, and a true number ten – alas, nothing was imminent. The manager would even go as far as to say journalists needed to take the questions to 'Mr Morris' for answers as he had submitted a list of transfer targets well before the January window had opened.

What made matters worse was a torn ACL for Krystian Bielik in the middle of January. Bielik was working his way back from a soft tissue injury and was playing for the under-23s when he twisted awkwardly under a challenge and suffered the injury. Cocu took some heat for the decision to play Bielik in the game – with some media and even the Poland manager calling it a 'meaningless fixture' – but the Dutchman defended his decision:

'It can happen in training, it can happen at any time. For him it was very important that he got back to playing games because he had been suspended and not playing a lot of minutes. He's still a young boy so he needs to play. This was a normal week for him playing on a Monday – lots of other players like Morgan [Whittaker] and Sibs [Louie Sibley] also played. But it is unfortunate and a very serious injury.'

Ultimately, the lack of inactivity was less a sign of Derby being slow to react in the market and more a sign that behind the scenes they knew something big was about to drop.

On 16 January 2020 the club was officially charged by the English Football League with breaching the financial regulations of the Championship following a review of the sale of Pride Park Stadium to Mel Morris. The EFL had initially launched an independent investigation into the sale in September 2019.

When quizzed about the ruling, Cocu was tight-lipped on the situation, 'I am not going into that subject now. I think it was a very clear statement from the club, so let's leave it at that. I don't like to go into details about it. Of course it is not pleasant for nobody, not only the players. A lot of people work at the club.'

In the same press conference it was also obvious that Cocu was trying to diplomatically offer up plausible reasons as to why Derby were waiting for reinforcements in the transfer window and why some may not be likely at all. However, one did not have to read the tea leaves when the recent announcement of the EFL's charge was being stuffed down your throat.

Internally, Derby were furious with the ruling. The club put out a strong statement, bullish and dripping with Morris's demeanour as internal communications people, and even some board members, asked him to reconsider the tone he was about to use. Alas, it was Morris's decision to push it through, wholeheartedly rejecting the claims and effectively declaring war on the EFL.

Morris bought the stadium through a new company, Gellaw Newco 202 Limited, for £81.1m according to Land Registry records, on 28 June 2018. Incidentally, that was two days before the 30 June year end for the club's 2017/18 financial accounts. The accounts published noted the sale of £81.1m had been made to 'companies under common ownership'. The sale was recorded as a £39.9m profit and it allowed the club to record a pretax profit of £14.6m. Had it not occurred, Derby would have recorded a loss of £25.3m.

Derby claimed they conducted their own independent commercial valuation of the stadium before selling it to Gellaw Newco 202; in fact, they claimed they had it valued twice just to be sure and when they had presented the valuation to the EFL, it is believed the governing body had no issues with the valuation at the time.

Derby had recorded losses of approximately £8m in 2016/17 and £14.7m in 2015/16. Teamed with the potential £25.3m loss which would have come without the sale of Pride Park, the club would have recorded total losses of

£48m over the three-year period, £9m over the £39m limit allowed to clubs if they were covered by their owner.

What the EFL were contending, as evidenced in the over-200-page written report after the fact, was that Pride Park Stadium, in their estimation, was worth £50m at the time when Morris effectively sold it to himself.

All of this felt like Morris's chickens coming home to roost. The owner had aggressively chased the Premier League dream and had seen transfer windows of mass spending while recouping very little in the way of sales. In 2015/16 Morris recruited heavily when bringing in Tom Ince, Bradley Johnson and Jacob Butterfield to name just three of the players who would contribute to a £30m window. However, those who left in that same window left on a free transfer, leaving the club £30m in the red for that season.

The following campaign was a little more balanced. Matěj Vydra and Ikechi Anya headlined a window spend totalling more than £15m while the club recouped a reported £14.4m in sales – largely thanks to Jeff Hendrick's departure to Burnley.

The 2017/18 season brought Derby's most profitable transfer window to that point. Academy product Will Hughes and forward Tom Ince were offloaded to Watford and Huddersfield Town respectively for a combined £16m amid a smattering of other outgoings and Derby sought to bring in cheaper options – such as Andre Wisdom, Tom Huddlestone and Curtis Davies. Tom Lawrence was the most expensive purchase at a shade under £5m. In total, the club banked a profit of just under £8m in the window.

Frank Lampard's transfer window proved to be one of the most costly in 2018/19. While Vydra's sale facilitated a £10m profit, Morris would once again spend heavily recruiting the likes of Martyn Waghorn, who himself joked that he was 'a snip' at £5m. Jack Marriott came in from Peterborough for around £3m after then Aston Villa manager John Terry gave Lampard a glowing recommendation for the striker after Villa played Posh in pre-season. Morris then outbid bitter rivals Leeds United to sign Florian Jozefzoon from Brentford. Leeds were keen to wrap up the signing for the winger, but were unwilling to pay more than their £2m bid. Derby leapfrogged the Yorkshire side with a bid of £2.75m. Duane Holmes also arrived for around £250,000. And then came the loans. Harry Wilson, Mason Mount and Fikayo Tomori were all on 'mate's rates' in terms of fees, but Derby still had to pay roughly £3.5m in loan fees for the trio as well as picking up a decent chunk of their wage packet. These were all just the headline acts of course – not to mention Ashley Cole turning up in January.

In all, the bill was hefty. And it was to the surprise of many. In the previous season, Morris and manager Gary Rowett couldn't come to an agreement on the funds available to replenish the squad. Morris was insistent that Rowett would have to sell players before he could bring anybody in, and Rowett wanted further ammunition to have a crack at getting into the Premier League. The two parted ways. But it was then a great shock to many to see Morris so free-flowing with the chequebook. This, of course, does not include the wages of the players. High-priced signings such as Waghorn were earning in the reported ballpark of £28,000 a week, the same as Ikechi Anya when he inked his four-year contract in 2016. Lawrence's contract was believed to pay him close to around £30,000 a week also. Some of the lowest earners in those windows came in at around £12,000 a week.

The EFL released a statement upon the charge, 'Following a review of Derby County's profitability and sustainability submissions, the EFL has charged the club for recording losses in excess of the permitted amounts provided for in EFL regulations for the three-year period ending 30 June 2018. The club will now be referred to an independent disciplinary commission, which will hear representations from the EFL and Derby.'

Derby retaliated with a strong statement of their own, claiming they 'adhered to the profit and sustainability rules' and adding, 'The stadium was subject to an independent professional valuation before sale, nearly 18 months ago, and the EFL indicated in writing the arrangement was in accordance with its rules and regulations. The EFL cannot now, long after approving the arrangements, suggest Derby County breached the rules.'

The sale ruffled the feathers of several EFL clubs, including Middlesbrough and their owner Steve Gibson, whose side missed out on a play-off place by a single point in 2018/19 – a place taken by Derby. Gibson, the EFL and Morris would be at loggerheads for the better part of two years, with the Boro chairman even threatening to sue the EFL over the sale of Pride Park.

Irked owners would not stop there as Wycombe Wanderers owner Rob Couhig was seeking compensation at the end of the 2020/21 season after claiming that the EFL failed to punish Derby on time – due to a series of appeals and counter-appeals which dragged the whole process out – resulting in Derby escaping a points deduction that campaign and relegating Wycombe by a single point. The potential punishment for Derby's financial mismanagement was at least nine points.

The sale of Pride Park was not the only charge the EFL levelled at Derby. There was a second charge relating to their amortisation policy of their players.

Amortisation is defined as the process of gradually writing off the initial cost of an asset. In football terms – a player's value will decrease over the course of their contract as it becomes closer to expiration. For example, if a player is bought for £20m and signed a four-year contract, after each year that player will lose £5m of their value in what is referred to as 'straight line' amortisation.

However, the EFL claimed that Derby changed their amortisation policy to gain more control of their amortisation costs but did not inform the league of this change. Instead, what Derby had chosen to do was amortise 'over the period of the respective players' contracts after consideration of their residual values'. Under this method the club had the chance to be creative with the figures to reduce the annual amortisation charge.

According to the Financial Reporting Standard FRS 102, a residual value of an intangible asset must be nil unless either:

- A third party has committed to purchase the asset at the end of its useful life, or
- There is an active market for the asset from which the residual value can be determined and which is

probable that such a market will be in existence at the end of the asset's useful life.

With that in mind, it suggested that Derby should not be using such a method for their players except in the following circumstances:

1. Derby have a third party committed to buying the player at the end of his useful life. This sounds reasonable, but surely at the end of a player's contract he is entitled to a Bosman transfer and so there would be no residual value, or

2. There is an active market for the asset. An active market is defined by accountants as 'a market in which transactions for the asset take place with sufficient frequency and volume to provide pricing information on an ongoing basis'.

It is believed that Morris felt he did nothing wrong other than find a legal loophole in the amortisation rules, insisting that the EFL had never said the club could not amortise in the manner he chose to, and that if there was a hard rule in place insisting on straight-line amortisation, the club would of course have followed it. As highlighted in the report, the club, or rather Morris, believed that the method of amortisation used did indeed comply with the EFL regulations.

Why this mattered so much is the belief that the accounting abnormality gave Derby an unfair advantage when it came to the overall spending limits imposed by the EFL – a claim Derby strongly refuted. Morris felt that the loophole was there for anybody to take advantage of, as the EFL had never explicitly stated that one did not have to use straight-line amortisation. Morris was angry with the EFL. His sentiment was that the EFL was trying to make an example out of Derby and hang the Rams out to dry for the governing body's own mess. Morris was also heavily irritated by what he believed were constant leaks to the press from the EFL – and had his suspicions as to who was leaking information, but preferred to keep his friends close and his enemies closer.

For the players, however, all of this was new and breaking right before their eyes. The club did not hold any meetings in the build-up to the decision, instead opting to brief the players after the fact, insist on their innocence and reassure players of their and Derby County's future. But it still left an uneasy feeling within the dressing room. Some of the players did not understand what it meant for them or the club – many believed what Morris and chief executive Stephen Pearce were telling them. Several high-ranking members of the squad felt it was as simple as an accounting issue and it would all get straightened out in the end and the club wouldn't face anything more severe than a hefty fine and perhaps a three-point suspended sentence. Regardless of the messaging after the fact, however, many players felt the higher-ups at the club should have kept them in the loop more.

'I found out on Twitter,' Curtis Davies said. 'I found out at the exact same time nearly everybody else found out. I'm not asking to be privy to big conversations with the higher-ups, but a heads-up would have been nice or a meeting with the lads to be transparent and tell us what was coming would have been nice. The way everything was handled with that … it just felt like something you shouldn't do. Felt like it could have been handled better.'

The club was effectively placed on ice for the next six months until the hearing had taken place – between 14 and 21 July.

In the report, details emerged of how the EFL's case was fought, particularly when it came to the valuation of Pride Park from one Roger Messenger, whom the report noted had very little stadia-valuing expertise – which it was keen to stress was not a criticism, but well worth noting.

Mr Messenger compared Pride Park to that of the Globe Arena of then-League Two Morecambe. The EFL, by the tone of writing in their report, were furious with this comparison and angry with Mr Messenger's defensive nature when cross-examined about the two stadiums, refusing to revise his valuation or comparison. The most glaring note was that 'the Globe is on any view inferior to Pride Park in its qualities and facilities' and also that the stadia only had one seated stand with the rest being covered terraces. They also highlighted the fact that the Globe had a capacity of just below 6,500, with a little over 2,200 seats – significantly less than the 30,000 Pride Park could seat.

Derby argued that the valuation of Pride Park was based on its 'rebuild cost' – if the stadium was to be destroyed, how much it would cost in the current economy to rebuild it as it was. Some of the findings valued the stadium at even higher than the £80m. The report stated:

'By reference to comparable stadia constructed between 1997 and 2018 and having consulted with its internal building cost team, a rate of £3,000 per seat is appropriate for construction of a modern equivalent of Pride Park stadium as at June 2018', giving an estimated rebuild cost as at June 2018 of just over £100m. The calculations at Appendix 6 of the Jones Lang Lassalle (JLL) report also 'bracketed' that figure with:

i) A 'Min rate' of £2,500 as cost per seat (equating to a minimum build cost for a modern equivalent of Pride Park of £83.6m), and

ii) A 'Max rate' of £3,500 as cost per seat (equating to a minimum build cost for a modern equivalent of Pride Park of £117.1m)

The report was so lengthy partly due to the complex nature of both charges and the intricate web Morris had woven to be constantly agile to get through whichever loopholes he felt were ready to exploit, but also in part due to his relationship with the governing body itself.

7

Morris v the EFL

MEL MORRIS and the EFL were often at loggerheads throughout the entirety of his reign as full owner, which began in 2015. Morris felt the governing body was not fighting hard enough for the clubs it represented and allowed the Premier League and broadcasters to often walk all over the lower divisions while EFL clubs would often creep into financial troubles. Morris also wanted the EFL to have a more stringent vetting process for potential owners – and even floated the idea of needing to apply for a licence to have football club ownership. From the EFL's perspective, they found Morris brash, difficult to deal with and willing to try anything to avoid interrogation and scrutiny. A frosty relationship became more fractured as Derby's problems worsened and the EFL probed further into their financial dealings and accounts, leading to Morris and the club hitting back with more and more fire each time – it got to such a distasteful and volatile point that, during the hearing of one of many appeals within the case, Morris said he believed he was being treated like the enemy of the EFL.

The EFL rebuked such an accusation in the formal written report of the hearing and declared:

'Regardless of how Mr Morris might perceive the way that he and the Club are viewed by the EFL, we reject any suggestion that the EFL's factual evidence was in any way tainted by animosity or dislike (and, for the avoidance of doubt, reject any suggestion that such animosity or dislike was established on the evidence before us), or that the EFL's factual evidence was in any way unreliable as a result.'

One of the biggest issues Derby's owner had was broadcasting revenue. Morris had long pushed hard for a bigger financial slice of the television income. It is believed that ticket sales accounted for around 30 per cent of Derby's annual income and, after Covid-19 especially, EFL clubs needed more money from TV deals so as not to rely so much on ticket sales to be sustainable. The way Morris saw it, without more money going to the EFL, many clubs would face extinction – something which he doubled down on in the wake of the pandemic and loss of mass revenue, which impacted EFL clubs more than many of the wealthy Premier League clubs, of which Morris would speculate ticket sales would only equate to around ten per cent of their total revenue.

It was also claimed that the EFL had to supplement Sky Sports' deal with the Premier League with no extra money going into their coffers for propping up the schedule if Sky Sports did not get their designated amount of televised matches that month. That incensed Morris, while he also pointed out that clubs with their own in-house streaming services for matches would also go black from time to time due to broadcasting regulations, another irritation because he saw it as the EFL trying to curtail how much its clubs could earn from their own means.

Morris had invested heavily in RamsTV, standing down potential investment in making a Derby County museum with much of the memorabilia the club's historian Andy Ellis had collected down the years, including parts of Brian Clough's old office, parts of the Baseball Ground, creepy dolls offered as gifts as part of a pre-season tour around the Czech Republic – standard stuff. Morris wished to have more eyes on the club and as part of that he saw its own in-house media and production crew, along with more content for the YouTube channels, essential. Owen Bradley, a former BBC journalist who often butted heads with Morris – which, conversely, earned him respect from Derby's owner – was brought in to spearhead the hosting duties of the project. Former Derby players would become freelance co-hosts alongside Bradley, including Michael Johnson and Shaun Barker.

Morris was hands-on with the project – often watching games on RamsTV to get a feel for the tone of the coverage – and would often provide his thoughts, usually wanting more uplifting analysis, as he would insist potential investors were watching the feed. When Derby were hammered 4-0 away at Cardiff City in March 2021, Johnson delivered a scathing assessment of the club and their chances of survival in the Championship. Johnson soon disappeared from RamsTV, and while the official line was that his time as a freelancer had come to an end, some felt the former skipper was stood down for making negative comments towards the club. Morris was also keenly aware of what was uploaded and said on the club's YouTube channel. In the early days of the 2019/20 season, a pilot featuring journalists aired but was quickly stomped out after Morris deemed some of the content critical of the club.

Morris also had issues with some of the top EFL executives, believing that some were not fit for purposes, had made too many past mistakes to remain credible or had an axe to grind with him personally. So deep was the mistrust that it even went into the official report of the EFL vs Derby charge when Morris went on record to say he felt he was an enemy of the EFL and that they had an axe to grind with him.

Morris and the EFL had been butting heads since the former had taken over Derby. In fact, not long after Morris had completed his takeover of the club, he set about trying to see an increase in broadcasting revenue and wrote a letter to all EFL clubs asking for their backing in the fight against the organisation. At the time, the Premier League was making £11m from a single televised game whereas the Championship was making around £600,000. Morris was calling on the EFL for more transparency and more say-so in how much money its clubs were given. Morris was even part of a cohort of owners – believed to be as many as 15 – which threatened a breakaway from the EFL in 2018 when again there was frustration over how much of the broadcasting revenue the EFL clubs would see from the five-year, £120m deal brokered. It was believed Championship clubs would pocket around £3m each.

That all formed a solid bedrock for a relationship riddled with tensions as Morris and the EFL did battle, and appealed, and counter-appealed, over the two charges, which would rumble on for two years.

8

Patience Wearing Thin

MEANWHILE, ON the pitch, Derby were beginning
to slide in the table. Between 5 October and 30 December
2019 they won just five out of 15 games, which included
a winless streak of seven between 26 November and a 2-1
victory over Charlton on the penultimate day of the year.
The skid had seen them drop from 14th to 17th in the
Championship. A seemingly outside chance of the play-
offs was soon having all the hallmarks of an undignified
relegation battle and murmurs were beginning to sound
out around Pride Park.

Phillip Cocu had tested the patience of fans on
more than one occasion already through the first half
of the season. The 3-0 hammering against bitter rivals
Nottingham Forest in the League Cup was the first time
in which he angered supporters for not understanding the
magnitude of the game – some never really forgave him
after that misstep – as well as the constant away defeats,
and not to mention the November loss at Forest in the
league when Derby never really threatened to worry Brice
Samba in the home side's goal.

Chief among the fans' irritations was the style of football, which had gone from being methodical with moments of incision to predictable and as slow as an ant pushing a brick across a desert. Supporters wanted more cut and thrust, more forward passes and less passing back to goalkeeper Kelle Roos. In fact, such was the frustration that fans would loudly boo when the ball was played back to Roos and he would take all the tempo out of the game instead of trying a quick outlet ball to get Derby on the transition.

Derby were among the lowest chance creators in the league, which resulted in them having one of the lowest numbers of shots and a worryingly meagre total of goals as they headed into the turn of the year. Derby would often dominate possession and would rank highly when it came to possessive passes – which never really threatened the opposition – but seldom cut through their opponents save for two or three instances a game. Then it would be the lack of a top-class finisher that would hamstring them. The mood was turning toxic.

To add to the tension was the emotion of a 14 December home clash against Millwall. Derby legend and former manager Jim Smith had passed away earlier in the week and the fans were in a collective mourning. The flag outside Pride Park was at half-mast, there was a minute's silence before the game and all staff and players sported the typical black armbands when such a loss befalls football. Smith was also on the cover of the matchday programme and inside former players who worked under the Bald Eagle gave testimony to his greatness. The whole ordeal brought with it a yearning for the old days from the fans. A feeling that Smith wouldn't have allowed Derby to play such stale football under his watch and be so passive in and out of possession. Smith was a symbol of what Derby could be at their apex – an exciting, attacking team with players from across the globe brought together under one roof and giving the big boys of the Premier League hell. His team had flavour, personality, charisma and steel in equal measure, while the 2019 Derby represented very little of that during their poor run of results. Fans were growing impatient of the playing style, of Cocu's platitudes in the media and generally how much hard work Derby made of things.

Compounding the emotions was that Millwall's manager was Gary Rowett. Rowett spoke before and after the game of his respect and love for Smith, having played under the Bald Eagle for the Rams in the 1990s. And there was the added bit of emotion – that Rowett was a former Derby manager and his Millwall side were chasing a promotion place.

The game was a poor one in truth – from both sides. But Millwall walked away the happier of the two as they won 1-0 thanks to a Tom Bradshaw goal. Derby dominated possession and had 11 shots but only one was on target. It continued a troublesome trend and at full time the fans were in no mood to forgive the latest subpar showing they'd just seen. The Pride Park faithful showered the team and manager with boos as they walked off the pitch and the anger was palpable.

'I observe and see we don't have enough courage to play,' Cocu assessed after the game. 'We kick it to Chris Martin and hope he can keep the ball. Then we conceded a goal which was not very well defended from us.'

Cocu pointed to a particular moment in the first half which literally had him throwing his head in his hands and turning away in disgust as Martyn Waghorn collected the ball on the left flank and spotted Max Lowe galloping ahead of him on the overlap into plenty of space – but Waghorn instead turned inside and played a safe pass backwards. It was a small incident that represented the overall safety-first approach which Derby players were opting to take. During a 3-0 defeat at Fulham on 26 November, Cocu often stood on the touchline shouting at his defensive line to push up, yet they would often sit five yards deeper than he wanted. So much so that during the game Cocu spent minutes on end waving his arm demanding his players push to at least the halfway line and when Krystian Bielik didn't follow orders Cocu waved his arms in despair and returned to his seat to chunter away at his two assistants.

Cocu pointed some of the finger at how Millwall set up after they scored the goal in the first half – withdrawing in their shape to five at the back with two screening midfielders and waiting for counterattacks. Derby in the second half probed and prodded but in truth never truly tested the Millwall defence even with their renewed efforts – it was more sizzle than steak with prettier build-up play but little dangers. In truth, it masked what was an overall poor effort.

What didn't help matters was two weeks later when a Wigan side struggling for form largely frustrated Derby, and the Rams were held to just seven shots all game and needed their final one – in the 93rd minute – to snatch a draw on yet another awful away day. The largest positive that was able to be taken out of the game was the fact that they hadn't lost. But the fans still voiced their displeasure at the lack of tempo in the passing and the lack of purpose for that matter, too. Only Wigan had scored fewer goals than Derby in the whole Championship heading into the game but they looked the more likely to find the net as Cocu's side continued to toil. It seemed the club as a whole was just desperate to get Wayne Rooney in the door to improve the goalscoring exploits, but it also threw up the question over whether the soon-to-be new Ram would be best placed as a midfielder – such was the lack of creativity from the middle of the park – in an effort to spice up Derby's approach play. After all, what use would it be bringing in one of the world's most prolific strikers if his team-mates couldn't get him the ball?

Coupling all of those frustrations with the club's EFL struggles and speculation as to how bad things could get – which did in fact become an eventuality with a 21-point deduction two seasons later – morale around the club was at a low point. The football wasn't fun for a lot of the players, the training sessions were long, the news cycle wasn't encouraging and Derby were looking at relegation rather than play-offs, which had been the goal when Cocu took charge and Rooney agreed to come on board in January. Now the man of the hour was arriving, and the staff had a different issue – where would he play?

9

Fitting in Rooney

AMID THE anger and confusion at the charge by the
EFL and the frustration of Derby's current position in the
Championship table as well as their poor displays on the
pitch, there was the not-so-small matter of finally seeing
Wayne Rooney on the pitch in Derby County colours.

The surreal nature of it all had not quite worn off.
Sky Sports had moved Derby's New Year's Day clash
with Barnsley to 2 January, in time for Rooney to be
registered so all cameras could be fixated on him.
Journalists from nearly every national outlet packed the
press box, emphasising the allure of one of England's
greatest footballers. Derby were 17th in the table at the
time while Barnsley propped up the division. The fixture
was otherwise unremarkable and there was no doubt that
without Rooney on the pitch its appeal would have been
tepid at best. The nation's media were not there to lust
over anybody else but England's and Manchester United's
all-time top goalscorer. The attendance figure even picked
up. Derby sold out Pride Park – and while the stadium
was often very full, ticket sales skyrocketed once Rooney's
debut game was confirmed. It all had to be viewed with

a slight grin that it was still 17th against 24th in the table with both teams entering the game in indifferent form. But Rooney had arrived – where would he play? How would he play? Would Championship football suit him? How much was still left in the tank? And was he really wearing a Derby County kit?

Of course Rooney was hoping to be joining the club in an effort to boost play-off hopes – maybe even the chances of Derby going up automatically or as champions. Instead he walked into a dressing room which was low on confidence and morale, a team which had only won once in their last eight matches and had only scored five goals in those games. The signing that was seen as someone who could take the team over the top and realise their Wembley dreams was instead sent on a rescue mission to save what was rapidly becoming a lost cause.

Rooney immediately elevated things upon his presence as players all fought hard to get in the team alongside a player who had accomplished just about everything there was to achieve in world football.

'I remember him turning up and thinking, "Wow – that's Wayne Rooney. I need to play with Wayne Rooney,"' midfielder Duane Holmes enthused. 'He wasn't quite the same as you remember him being at Man United, but then he was older. But you could still see his quality, you could still tell he had it mentally with how quick he'd pass the ball.'

'I was in awe of him when he first came in,' defender Max Lowe said. 'It's Wayne Rooney, isn't it. We're all wondering what he's doing at Derby County but at the same time buzzing he is here. And immediately the boys started pushing more in training – sometimes you wondered where that level of intensity was before he showed up.'

One of the first things which caused a slight stir was taking the captain's armband off Curtis Davies and giving it to Rooney. An obvious choice to many, but the move to take the accolade away from one of the club's most dedicated and professional servants stung for some team-mates and signalled an early sign that Rooney would be treated differently to the rest of the players. Davies himself had no issues with handing over the captaincy to Rooney. The former Aston Villa centre-back was not the first choice as skipper to begin with after Richard Keogh's sacking, only securing the armband after Tom Huddlestone was stripped of it having only held it briefly following the fateful Joiner's Arms night. As far as Davies was concerned, he was never the chosen player to begin with.

'Obviously it was a bit like a hot potato with the armband,' he said. 'It went from Rich, to Tom, and then to me. So I never really felt like the manager wanted me as captain to begin with. I think it was more to do with politics and image after the car crash incident – I was a calm, senior player. But obviously Phillip always wanted to get rid of me, so he never saw me as a true captain. And I wasn't too fussed. I didn't need an armband to lead. It's cliche but you need 11 leaders on the pitch in one way or another.'

Rooney's introduction and special treatment was not an issue for those around the club in the early days – especially in the immediate aftermath of him joining.

'He's Wayne Rooney – at one point in time maybe the best player in the world. Certainly one of the best the Premier League has ever seen,' one former coach put it.

'And with that comes special treatment – and that's fine when you're playing well and he's playing well. But it's a dangerous game to play when things start to turn – and I think Phillip found that out.'

When it came to Rooney's position, it was more up in the air than one might have expected considering he made his name as one of the great strikers of his generation, but in his later years he had regressed to deeper roles on the pitch, turning more facilitator than scorer. At his initial introductory press conference the previous August, Rooney and Cocu were both noncommittal on where the former Manchester United and England captain would be deployed, declaring it would be on a situational basis determined by various factors.

Rooney could fill two voids Derby so desperately needed – creativity in the middle of the pitch, and goals. Cocu said as much in December when asked about his plans for the January window.

'Goals,' he asserted when asked what he'd like to add. 'The struggle we have had all season is finding the net. We can't think we get Wayne Rooney in January and everything will be fine, I don't think that's enough. For the building process for the second part of the season and also for next season, it's very important we make the right move.'

Rooney would be deployed in a deeper role in midfield, next to Max Bird, and would spray passes across the field for his team-mates to run on to. The early signs were bright as Derby now had a clear creative spark in the middle of the pitch, but the profligacy in front of goal still remained and Rooney would often push up to play as the striker – the problem being the service would then experience a serious drop-off and he would become isolated at the top end of the pitch with nary a chance to slot away.

Cocu would later reveal that the plan was originally to play Rooney as a central striker but he also recognised that his team lacked the creativity to service him sufficiently enough, and therefore he would have to turn provider – a suboptimal way to use a record-breaking goalscorer at club and international level but, nonetheless, things were going well in the early stages.

Questions were also often asked of Cocu's hesitancy to select Jack Marriott more consistently. The striker had earned himself talisman status after his heroics the previous season for Frank Lampard, but had started in just six games for Cocu before the turn of the year – playing 90 minutes in half of those. In fact Marriott would start only one more game after the new year, a 2-1 away defeat to Queens Park Rangers, and would add just one more goal to his tally – the opener in a 2-1 home win over Barnsley, assisted by the debuting Rooney.

Such was Marriott's frustration heading into the turn of the year that he was open to moving away from the club to seek game time, with Hull City testing the waters – Marriott had a good relationship with then Tigers manager Grant McCann after their successful stint together at Peterborough United. However, Derby were reluctant to sell for anything less than the £3m they had paid for Marriott 18 months earlier and had no interest in allowing him to go out on loan.

There were questions as to whether Marriott fitted in Cocu's style and system. The striker was tried in an array of shapes and positions from being the lone striker up front to being part of a pair in a diamond formation to even playing out on the wing – but nothing ever seemed to click with him. Marriott offered speed in behind, which peers Rooney, Chris Martin and Martyn Waghorn could not, an out ball on the counterattack and was perhaps the most natural number nine the squad had.

Yet fitness issues always plagued him. After the 1-1 Boxing Day stalemate against Wigan, Cocu shed some light on the restrictions to Marriott's playing time:

'The goal for us all, including Jack, which is why I put him on for 30 minutes – it was something he could handle after being out recently with a small injury. But that happens quite a lot. A certain period in the season he played five or six games [in a row] but then he had an injury again. He has certain qualities that we need in the team.

'But he also has to work on his physical state so he can bring what he brings for a longer period of time. And last season he had the same problem. And that's a struggle at the moment, to find a balance of what he can handle on loads and in sessions and in games.'

The final comment about Marriott's 'physical state' ignited the touchpaper that he was injury-prone. Adding more fuel to the fire was Rooney's public criticism of Marriott after the former's debut against Barnsley. In a game in which Marriott could have had a hat-trick before half-time, he had to settle for just the one goal. Afterwards, Rooney spoke with Sky Sports about his debut and the team performance as a whole and he was less than impressed with his team-mate – though he delivered his words with a smile, possibly in a bid to soften the blow:

'It's not that he missed – obviously players miss chances
– it was the way he was casual and lazy with it. I said to
him at half-time and he said he thought he was offside,
and I think it's something he will learn off. Go through,
put the ball in the back of the net and if you are offside,
so be it. You score the goal. Hopefully he won't be doing
that again.'

The criticism stung Marriott and those close to him.
Several players who got on well with the striker saw
opinions on his character from the outside as unfair and
without any evidence whatsoever, while comments from
Rooney and the manager could have been made behind
closed doors so as to protect Marriott from further criticism
from the public.

Marriott himself even addressed the allegations and
criticisms levelled at him on the *JuddyTalks* podcast in
July 2020, not long after football had resumed following a
three-month hiatus during the Covid-19 pandemic.

'It got to a stage where it wasn't necessarily just
affecting my physical health, it was affecting me mentally
as well,' he revealed. 'Because when you're a striker and
all you want to do is some extra finishing or some extra
training and every time you shoot on your right foot you
feel that your stomach is just going to rip apart. It's awful
because you feel that you then can't work on your game
and your improvements because every time you do this
particular thing.

'Mentally that affects you, because you then think
"How is this going to get any better?" in the meantime
while waiting for the operation. That was the biggest
difficulty – I am reading all these tweets and people

are saying "injured, injured, injured, X, Y and Z". People are making perceptions of you as a character and you as a person. I think mentally that was hard, trying to force yourself through it just to get to the end of the season.

'That's from nothing, that's just a creation of nothing when you're working so hard to try and get back on the pitch. You're actually having to stop doing finishing sessions because you're in that much pain. That's not good.

'And then you're getting tweets and you're getting perceived as "this" – that you don't work hard and you're not trying.'

Marriott was not present when the club returned to training as football resumed in the summer of 2020, due to him recovering from groin surgery. The problem had been niggling away since September, but the decision was made to hold off surgery and instead treat the injury with a series of injections and painkillers in the hopes that surgery would be possible at the end of the season – a decision which some of the players criticised and attributed to holding Marriott back throughout the season.

'The amount of medication and tablets I was taking just to play with the pain was unbelievable. I've been taking all sorts of pain relief to get through a game, but yet every time you kick the ball with your right foot you are feeling this awful pain at the very bottom of your stomach and it was just so uncomfortable,' Marriott said. 'It got to the stage where at the start of lockdown we tried to get the surgery in, but all the hospitals shut down to help the NHS – rightly so. So it was a case of holding off and I spent the whole lockdown waiting for the surgeon.'

Another thing working against Marriott was indeed the passive style of play the team had been playing. If using Marriott's speed to stretch the opposition defence behind was the plan, then slowing down the pace of the game actively hampered his ability to do just that and allowed defenders to drop off and cut off the space in behind. Marriott would often have long balls kicked up towards him to chase after but so often it was futile. Try as he might, Marriott was no target man to make the ball stick, and defenders were often so deep that there was no space for him to run into and exploit.

As well as Marriott's own fitness concerns, there were now question marks over the status of Derby's recently acquired talisman. Prior to the pandemic shutting football down for three months, Rooney had provided four goals and two assists in 12 games in a midfield role. His quick feet, ability to anticipate where passes needed to be for runners to get on the end of and aggression in playing between the lines made the Rams a much more potent force when going forward. Mix in his deadly ability from set pieces and it appeared that Derby could muster an unlikely play-off charge with Rooney taking centre stage. His post-pandemic play would start what would become a decline in his general performances, however, not helped by the lack of support around him.

When training resumed, Rooney looked unfit. So much so that even some of his team-mates felt he was not worthy of a place in the side and that he was now clearly being picked on name and reputation. Photographs even circulated showing Rooney in the game before football stopped and in his first training session back in June and it seemed he had put on some weight. Though he scored a goal in two out of the first three games – one a penalty against Reading in a 2-1 home win, another a free kick in a 1-0 victory at Preston North End – they masked largely deflating performances.

Rooney would end the season with six goals and three assists in all competitions and was a large driving force behind Derby mustering a brief play-off push which went as close as them being one point off the top six, but a run of four defeats on the spin, three of those to teams in the top six (Leeds, Brentford and West Bromwich Albion), meant their hopes were dashed almost as quickly as they were ignited.

While his impact during his half season in a Derby shirt could be considered a resounding success, a growing problem was developing within the squad – a question of favouritism. Rooney was of course the star attraction, the captain and the most accomplished footballer to turn out for the club perhaps since the late 1970s. He had cultivated a reputation – rightly so – as one of the best of his generation, if not of all time. With that came certain perks, but also certain irritations from the squad.

'When we lost to QPR,' Max Lowe begins, 'he tries a cross-field ball and leaves it so short and they pick up the ball. I've pushed up the pitch and was sprinting back to try and stop the goal and he's jogging slowly. I started well ahead of him and by the time the goal goes in I'm inside the box and he's on the edge of the area. When we get into the changing room Cocu turns to me and chews me out for being so far up the pitch – even though we were attacking and I was told to push up when we had the ball. He didn't say a word to Wayne. Even though he lost the ball and then didn't really bust a gut to track back. Things like that made some of the boys feel like Wayne was untouchable.'

Those slack passes and lack of legs to track back would slowly creep into Rooney's game until they were a constant frustration.

Rooney's performances on the pitch declined further still at the start of the 2020/21 season. This time he was playing more as the central striker following the departure of Chris Martin, who had left to join Bristol City at the end of the season following a stalemate in contract negotiations with the Rams. The problems which occurred when Rooney played up front in the previous season once again reared their head. Rooney often cut an isolated and frustrating figure. He would regularly roam from his position deeper just to get touches of the ball and get involved in the game.

When he had to miss three games due to coming into close contact with somebody who had contracted Covid-19, Derby drew two and lost one, but overall their performances looked better, prompting the question as to whether Rooney should return to the starting XI at all.

During the absence, Cocu had switched to a 3-4-3 formation and the team looked more fluid and comfortable in their assignments. They even stuck to it upon Rooney's return and gained a 1-1 draw against Bournemouth – a game in which they took the lead early before surrendering a late equaliser. However, for the next match, a 1-0 home defeat to Queens Park Rangers, Cocu reverted back to the old 4-2-3-1 system, irritating some of the players who saw it as a way to crowbar Rooney back into the side. The performance was lifeless and Rooney struggled to make any impact, often flitting between midfielder and attacker in a bid to make something happen as Derby tried to battle their way out of the relegation zone and Cocu's seat heated up intensely.

10

They Couldn't – Could They?

DERBY ROLLED into 2020 off the back of a 2-1 victory over Charlton Athletic. It was a hard-fought win which was achieved with backs against the wall after Krystian Bielik received a straight red card on 17 minutes following a wild challenge, but a Jason Knight double set Derby on their way. Wayne Rooney was in the technical area for the first time as a coach, forming an early prequel to his formal debut against Barnsley three days later. But for all the effort, the feel-good factor of an academy boy grabbing the goals and for Rooney being an official part of the team now, Derby still sat 17th and were nine points off the play-offs but had previously shown no sign that they would be capable of putting together a run to close that gap. Their best unbeaten run prior to the turn of the year was five games – and three of those were draws. Since that time they had specialised in winning one only to then lose their following match prior to their seven-game winless run starting at the back end of November.

The victory against Charlton signalled the start of five wins in seven games and propelled Derby from 17th to 13th. Rooney's impact on the team during their impressive run of form could not be overstated. He contributed two goals and two assists, but more than that he made the Rams quicker in attack. Rooney's fanciful feet, quick brain and laser-accurate passing turned Derby from an often plodding, methodical and sometimes boring outfit into a team with real incision, decisiveness and an ability to turn teams in the blink of an eye. While Max Bird, Bielik and Knight were all quality central midfielders, Rooney processed the game a second quicker allowing the midfield to suddenly become a hub of creativity.

Perhaps no two games summed up what Derby and Rooney at their best could be more than a 4-0 home thrashing of Stoke City followed up by a gritty come-from-behind 3-2 victory at Swansea City which put a halt to their away woes. During both matches Derby were ruthless in transition, moving the ball from front to back with remarkable speed, quick passing and good decision-making. At the heart of that was Rooney – and he sprinkled even more stardust with a superb free-kick goal against Stoke. To what degree Rooney lifted everybody's performance around him is debatable, but what isn't up for discussion is how nearly all of the squad hit a purple patch.

During those five wins in seven matches Duane Holmes bagged two goals – both crucial equalisers, during the 2-2 draw against Middlesbrough and then again in the 3-2 win over Swansea to get the score back to 2-2 – and laid on a pair of assists. It was his most productive portion of the season and the period when Holmes felt he was playing his best football right before he broke his leg against Huddersfield in February.

'I was playing down the middle – which is where I feel my best position is,' Holmes said. 'I'd been starting and finishing 90 minutes, I was feeling fit and confident and you could see all the boys were starting to come out of their shell. We put together a good run and we were getting more confident each game. Obviously for me that all went away when I broke my leg – which was a shame.'

Holmes had spent a lot of the season as a utility player but with him spending less time on the right wing, as Cocu liked to use him, there was space for Martyn Waghorn to fill in there – as well as do a job as a centre-forward when Chris Martin was being rested. Waghorn possessed a powerful left foot, a willingness to chase and press from the front and was no slouch when it came to taking a mean set piece either. His post on the right as an inside-forward coincided with a purple patch of his own in which he netted five goals and logged four assists from the turn of the year until the end of the season – although his final goal came in February, he did score four goals and lay on one assist during the seven-game stretch which saw Derby shoot up the table. Waghorn was often self-deprecating in his assessment of his own ability and his own form throughout the season. He would often reference how he felt he should have scored more goals – even though he would be the club's joint top scorer along with Martin with 12 – and would place heavy emphasis on other aspects of his job which made the team a cohesive unit when playing well. Rooney's arrival on the pitch, as well as the pair forming a bond off it, signalled a huge upswing in form for the former Rangers striker who played no small part in hauling Derby out of the potential relegation battle they were in.

The second half of the season also saw Jason Knight rocket towards instant starter status within the squad. Prior to his two-goal heroics against Charlton in late December 2019, he had yet to score a senior goal. With Rooney in the building, Knight would score six goals during his debut senior season and provide one assist. The Irishman continued to be used across Derby's midfield but thrived regardless of position. His sublime performance against Charlton came when deployed as a number ten, while his excellent display in the away win against Sheffield Wednesday came with him mostly occupying the right-wing spot, and his energetic efforts during the 3-0 thrashing of Blackburn Rovers right before football stopped for three months was carried out on the left.

Another benefactor of the Rooney effect was Chris Martin. Despite being in and out of the team depending on the opposition and how Cocu wished to set up tactically, Martin scored seven of his 11 league goals after Rooney's arrival and would also add a hat-trick of assists during the 3-1 victory over the Owls at Hillsborough. Martin's ability to make the balls stick when played up to him, work the channels and also drop into midfield to link the play was a terrific foil for the playmaking Rooney who, prior to lockdown, was fully pulling the strings for a team now purring along with fewer splutters.

Perhaps no member of the squad benefitted from Rooney's influence more than Tom Lawrence. Prior to Rooney's arrival, Lawrence had scored five goals and notched one assist, in 2019/20. It was not a bad return, but that four of those goals came across two games – a double in the opener at Huddersfield Town and both goals in a 2-0 home victory over Middlesbrough – meant that Lawrence had only had a direct goal involvements in four games before the turn of the year. That was not nearly enough for a player with such ability, but he was also suffering for many months following the fallout from the drink-driving incident. Upon his return from a two-game suspension for picking up ten yellow cards – something Phillip Cocu said was 'too much' for an attacking player – Lawrence grabbed assists in successive games and would find the net five more times too, including a stunning winner against Swansea and a brace against Sheffield Wednesday.

Derby were now starting to resemble a team with a clear identity when in possession, but still had their moments of malfunctioning and making life tough for themselves – old habits die hard as they say. The team could often go from being quick as a whippet to being infuriatingly one-paced which meant they barely laid a glove on the opposition. But the Rooney effect had papered over many cracks. Yet for all of that recent upswing in form, Derby still had a significant gap to close when it came to pushing for the play-offs. Five wins from seven games meant the deficit was reduced from nine points to seven – progress in the table was looking slow even if on the field it was now happening at a more accelerated pace.

But Derby couldn't help but fall back into their similar pattern – this time a four-match winless streak which set back their play-off hopes. It was in this run that February's frustrating 3-2 loss to Bristol City – having been 3-0 down – and a 1-1 draw against Huddersfield Town were played out. Individual mistakes cost Derby more than ten goals throughout Cocu's only full season and though the players bore most of the blame, it was the coaching style the Dutchman insisted upon that some players struggled to adapt to, meaning getting more flustered when under pressure and leading to the mistakes. In short – both parties were responsible, even if the goals went down as player errors.

In light of the winless streak, however, Derby found new grit and resilience. They dismantled Sheffield Wednesday with a first-half blitz which saw them 3-0 up inside 30 minutes. It was arguably their most complete half under Cocu with all the hallmarks of what he was trying to create. Lawrence and Knight ran the show that afternoon and the overall professional performance gave Cocu something to smile about.

'We found a good combination and balance in playing good football and being effective,' he said after the win. 'With a score of 3-0 we had to make sure they couldn't get back in the game and we made changes to get some fresh energy and control – and it's pleasing to keep control after almost a perfect first half.'

The result would begin a run of five straight league wins – albeit with a three-month gap in between them – during which time Derby found different ways to win matches, from blowing opponents away to outscoring them in high-scoring affairs and grinding games out after taking an early lead.

Of course, sandwiched in between those games was an FA Cup run which the Rams were pursuing with great energy. Derby had knocked off Crystal Palace at Selhurst

Park in the third round thanks to a Chris Martin goal and needed a replay at home to dispatch Northampton Town 4-2 – after drawing 0-0 in the away fixture – ultimately earning a place in the fifth round. Naturally, the football and narrative gods read the tea leaves and gave the broadcasters, media and fans what they wanted – Derby County vs Manchester United. The Wayne Rooney appreciation match. The entire build-up was centred around Rooney, now captain of Derby County, trying to thwart a Manchester United team, managed by Ole Gunnar Solskjær, which failed to resemble so many dominant United sides Rooney had been a part of. It was about the past – Rooney's relationship with Sir Alex Ferguson, with Solskjær as a team-mate. It was about the present – how big of a chance was it for Derby to beat a United team yet to fully click, and extend their cup run? How far off vintage United sides were Solskjær's iteration of the Red Devils? And it was of course about the future – would Rooney one day like to manage the club where he became an icon?

Outside of the natural narrative, however, were equally interesting subplots – such as Max Bird and Jason Knight both growing up Manchester United fans and now being key parts to a team squaring off against them in one of English football's most romanticised competitions.

'I used to shout Rooney's name from the stands, I had his name on the back of my United shirt,' Bird said in a June 2020 interview with The Athletic. 'Playing alongside him, in that game particularly, I knew I had to train well that week to get into the side for the game because that opportunity might not happen again.'

The tie was a routine 3-0 win for Manchester United in which the latter stages became more a testimonial for Rooney – some fans even annoyed when United goalkeeper Sergio Romero stopped an on-target Rooney free kick from flying into the top corner. No matter – the result was disappointing but did not impact the Rams' league form.

A 3-0 thumping of Blackburn Rovers got Derby back on track as the Championship welcomed Louie Sibley. Sibley marked his first league start with a 25-yard thunderbolt which set Cocu's side on their way to a dominant victory in what would be their last match before football's Covid-enforced hiatus. When matches returned in June, with no fans present, a Sibley hat-trick against Millwall was required as Derby ran out 3-2 winners in a game that never once threatened to slow the pace in an end-to-end encounter which, for the most part, had not favoured Derby all season. Rooney then scored from the penalty spot in a 2-1 home win over Reading, and added a free kick as the Rams gritted out a 1-0 victory over Preston North End. The five-match winning streak in the league shot Derby up the table from 15th to seventh and with just one single point between themselves and Cardiff City, who were occupying the final play-off spot.

'It's looking positive. We've come a long way,' Cocu said after the Preston victory. 'In this stage of the season to be in that position and that it's still possible for us – that's something we've worked very hard for. To be playing games that could maybe get us into the play-offs it's a big bonus for the team and extra motivation for us.'

The Rams were rolling into their home East Midlands derby fixture against Nottingham Forest in fine form.

Their bitter rivals were also playing well since Project Restart, notching a draw and back-to-back wins. Forest under Sabri Lamouchi had become a tough nut to crack defensively while being one of the better counterattacking teams in the Championship. Derby were also out to rectify their 1-0 loss to the Reds in November and with revenge would come a further strengthening of their play-off push while denting fourth-placed Forest's own ambitions.

To add extra motivation for the Derby squad, Andre Wisdom came in to visit the team not even a week after he had been stabbed in his head and buttocks while visiting family in Liverpool. His injuries were serious but not life-threatening.

'It was very good to see him. It was especially good for the lads,' Cocu said in the build-up to the match. 'It was a big shock for everybody and had a big impact on the team. When he visited us it was a big boost for the team – it was really good to see him.'

Of course Derby would have to face their bitter rivals without a crowd due to Covid-19 – a bitter pill to swallow as some players Cocu alluded to needed a big crowd to get them fired up and to add extra intensity to their performance. Not to mention the fans being cruelly robbed of playing such a big part of such a pivotal derby clash with play-off implications. Nevertheless, there was a job to do and the squad was prepared to push Forest to the limit in an effort to boost their own top-six hopes and spoil the chances of their rivals.

'It's a different game in the fact that we don't have our fans with us. We'll miss them for sure. The atmosphere of the fans can influence a game, your own team, your opponent, the referees, in such a big game they're an important part of it – we'll have to find a way to deal with that and it's not an excuse for us,' said Cocu. 'They [Forest] know if they get a good result against us, it almost guarantees them a play-off place. And for us as well we can strengthen our own play-off hopes – and we'll give it a good go.'

The match itself was a fairly tame affair – not helped by the fact it was played in near silence save for the screams and yelps of players and coaching staff. Forest grabbed an early lead through Joe Lolley and then set about suffocating Derby's midfield to cut off any and all supply to the forwards. Crucially, of course, they hounded Rooney and Sibley – ensuring neither could find any rhythm in the game and forced them into risky passes and dribbles to create turnovers. The method restricted Derby to just two shots on target entering the final six minutes of injury time – where the game would take three incredible turns.

Firstly, in the 94th minute Waghorn was sent off for a studs-up challenge – born out of frustration – on Ryan Yates. The dismissal looked to be the final nail in the Rams' coffin as just a minute and a half of added time remained, they were down to ten men and Forest had the ball with a chance to run down the clock.

With the final seconds slipping away, Derby won a free kick just inside the Forest half and Rooney tossed it in accurately, yet hopefully. Every outfield Derby player except him was in the Forest penalty area. Brice Samba came out to try and deal with the swirling ball but flapped at it and Chris Martin headed home a knock-back which crawled over the line with all eyes on the referee to check if his wristwatch had vibrated to signal the ball was over – it did, and Derby were level with the final kick of the match. Cocu celebrated wildly with Shay Given and pandemonium was out on Pride Park as Derby kept their play-off hopes fully alight.

Thirdly – and most hilariously – was a Nottingham Forest fan throwing himself into a canal in celebration of his team's victory, only to be hauled from the water by police and told that, in fact, Derby had grabbed a last-second leveller.

Cocu was proud of the point his side had managed to snatch given the flow of the game but was annoyed in the manner his side equipped themselves throughout the opening exchanges:

'In my opinion they're one of the best teams in the league – compact, hard to beat, and they can play excellently on the counterattack. It's a big, big point for us. We were slow at the start of the game, we hesitated and not aggressive – it changed after we conceded a goal but that also disappointed me because we shouldn't have to concede a goal to wake up.'

Wake up the Rams did not, however. Their next four games came against sides all in the top six – West Bromwich Albion, Brentford, Cardiff City and eventual champions Leeds United. Derby were soundly beaten in all four while only really being competitive in the 2-1 loss at Cardiff. Across the four matches they lost by an aggregate of 10-3 and registered just seven shots on target.

Perhaps most upsetting to the fans was the 3-1 home defeat against a much-changed and heavily hungover Leeds side – who had been celebrating their promotion to the

Premier League the night before, after West Brom lost at Huddersfield. Marcelo Bielsa's team were sluggish by their own standards in the first half, and early in the second half they allowed Derby to take the lead through Martin. That woke the Yorkshire side up, however, and they proceeded to pull the hosts apart with ease and register a victory which confirmed their status as champions and meant they drank champagne and paraded all over Pride Park. It was a bit of payback for the previous season's Derby play-off semi-final celebrations at Elland Road and a bitter pill to swallow for the Rams.

Derby ended the season on a high by beating Birmingham City 3-1 at St Andrew's to secure a top-ten finish, but in earnest they soon began their work for 2020/21 when they wished to model themselves after two teams who'd just put them to the sword – Brentford and Leeds.

11

Covid Puts a Halt to Things

BY THE time March 2020 had arrived, world news was being dominated by Covid-19. Countries had already begun to put measures in place and precautions were at an all-time high – even in the press room several journalists were refusing to shake hands and were using scarves, snoods or even their jumpers as makeshift face masks. Elsewhere, in Austria, Derby's youth team had travelled for their UEFA Youth League last-16 tie against RB Salzburg. The players were aware of the goings-on around the world but also, at a time when the UK had no restrictions at all, didn't feel the need to take any extra precautions until they got more of a picture as to what was going on – of course people were still figuring out what the symptoms of Covid were and how best to avoid contracting it. The threat of airport closures had not yet reached the UK, making travel into and out of the country routine. But things would ramp up shortly after.

Fresh off the back of a 3-1 away victory against Sheffield Wednesday and a 3-0 home demolition of Blackburn Rovers, Derby were looking to mount a late play-off charge in the final quarter of the season. They had produced a masterful opening half an hour against the Owls and blew them away by scoring three times before professionally seeing out the job in the second half. Against Blackburn they picked up where they left off and were buoyed by Sibley's thunderbolt on his first Championship start. It seemed that Phillip Cocu's philosophy had finally clicked; the smattering of young players looked fully settled and Wayne Rooney was finally in the side and making a difference.

During this time, however, Covid-19 was spreading globally and conversations were starting to be had as to whether football would – or even should – continue. Derby were set to face Millwall on 15 March but in the lead-up to the game news broke that Nottingham Forest's owner Evangelos Marinakis had tested positive for the virus and had also met with senior Millwall figures during Forest's clash with them the previous weekend. Despite this news the EFL insisted that Derby's away clash with the Lions was in no danger of being postponed – there wasn't any official government guidance at this point as the world scrambled to figure out the most effective solution. Derby contacted both the EFL and Millwall to seek clarification on the situation but nothing was forthcoming. Two days before the fixture it was postponed in line with government restrictions. All games would be cancelled until at least 3 April when the situation would be reassessed. However, no football would take place until late June as the UK went into a full lockdown.

The extended break was both a bizarre and welcome one for many of the squad. Duane Holmes used lockdown to deal with a bout of depression after losing his best friend and breaking his leg in the space of a month – the time alone in his house meant he had 'no choice but to deal with it'.

For players such as Martyn Waghorn, it presented a chance to spend more time with his family which he greatly enjoyed.

'It's been a bizarre three or four months to be honest,' Waghorn said prior to Derby's Project Restart clash against Millwall. 'The first period of it [lockdown] was brilliant for me. As footballers you don't get to spend the time that many people do with their families day in, day out. So I've loved spending time with my wife, and my son, and all the stuff he's doing at school – took me back to my youth.

'Then just being in the garden with my family, painting together. It was difficult at times, don't get me wrong. But I enjoyed large parts of it because I got to be with my family. Then I found out we were going to be having a second child and that gave us a lot of energy and encouragement to get through the tough period.'

Next on the docket for the club was wage deferrals. Clubs across the country had been deferring wages for many of their playing and non-playing staff, some even laying staff off, to cope with the financial strain the pandemic placed on them. Originally Derby higher-ups wanted all players to take a 50 per cent deferral – which wouldn't be paid back until 2021 – in a bid to limit the financial damage. The proposal was rejected outright by the players and the PFA before Mel Morris and all the players got together on a Zoom meeting to discuss it further. Wayne Rooney got much of the credit for instigating a fairer deal, but many pointed to Curtis Davies. Waghorn was just as instrumental in getting a fair offer and speaking up for his fellow team-mates. Finally an agreement was reached in which players would defer on a case-by-case basis, anywhere from 25 per cent up to 50 per cent depending on what they could spare.

In a statement the club said:

'Derby County Football Club has today confirmed that all first-team players, football management, executives and non-furloughed staff have agreed to take wage deferrals as part of the ongoing response to the coronavirus pandemic.

'First-team players have voluntarily agreed a substantial deferral that is considerably more than has been reported in the media, while Phillip Cocu and his coaching team, and chief executive officer Stephen Pearce and his staff have also agreed significant deferrals.

'In addition, players, coaches and staff have made financial donations to the club's Stay Safe, Stay Fit, Stay Connected campaign, and non-playing club staff are volunteering their time to operate the food hub set up at Pride Park Stadium and deliver food to where it is most needed across the city.

'Talks across the club have been held in the spirit of unity and co-operation, and everyone has been fully committed to help and play their part. The club would specifically like to thank Wayne Rooney, the team captain, and Curtis Davies, the Professional Footballers' Association's club representative, for their help and support.

'The measures have been agreed as part of the ongoing work to protect the future of the club, our staff and the communities we serve, during these unprecedented times.'

Negotiations were not smooth sailing, however.

'It felt like things would change at the last minute all the time,' Max Lowe said. 'Originally we thought it was going to be 30 per cent, and it would be paid back to us in instalments after six months. Then at the last minute it changed to being 50 per cent across the board. Then it would change again.'

'The negotiations were difficult because we'd never been in that situation before,' Davies added. 'But some of the conversations that were happening were a bit forceful. And then there were a lot of 11th-hour conversations. We could have a chat about where we were at as a club, accountants would come in and tell us where we were at, then the PFA's independent accountants would come in and see the club's finances and see a rough figure of what a deferral would be ... we go through all of this and then at the 11th hour, they'd demand more changes. It would go from 25 per cent to 50 per cent just like that.

'We'd be getting told what other clubs have done – 30 per cent, 35 per cent – and being told that around that ballpark would be good. Then we were all told to do it individually and if we wanted a chat with Mel and Stephen Pearce then to reach out because obviously we've all got separate financial situations. It felt like the goalposts were always being shifted. I don't hold any grudge against the club because of that because it's a situation we'd never faced. You needed to ask players to ask them to take a wage deferral. Some clubs were taking full-time wage cuts so we were trying to play ball so it was just a deferral because if the club went under, we've got nothing.

'It was difficult because at a time when we were all supposed to come together, it felt like the players were being pitted against each other. Which was a shame. But once it was all resolved we got on with it. I didn't hold a grudge against the club for it.'

The club were trying to find a way to pay back the deferrals and one way in which they believed they could bankroll it was through sales, the most high-profile of which were Jayden Bogle and Max Lowe, who were sold to Sheffield United for a total fee of £12m in September 2020.

'We were told by the club that the money they received for us was going to go towards paying back the deferrals,' Lowe said. 'As far as I'm aware, that never happened or it did, but not at the previously agreed rate.'

Cocu voluntarily deferred half of his wages in an effort to help the club before spearheading several community initiatives within the community. Cocu was at the heart of Stay Safe, Stay Fit, Stay Connected.

'It's a way we try to help and support the community in Derbyshire,' Cocu said to RamsTV. 'Our fans have always been very loyal in their support to us, so we worked on a project to try to help the community in as many ways as possible. The Stay Safe part is in conjunction with the Derby Community Trust – we send food packages to the most vulnerable and most in need in Derbyshire. We also have a food hub in Pride Park for people to be able to make food donations for those in need.

'Stay Fit is about workouts made by players and our physical staff. It's three times a week, it's to help us all stay healthy in a physical way and also a mental way. And stay connected is about connecting in various ways by having a little bit of fun with families and players. But also they are connected throughout the community with involvement from the players and staff. We set up a week on our website where Curtis Davies is meeting fans – Craig Forsyth is also helping and we have Shay Given to talk about non-coronavirus issues. We're trying to stay connected with our fans and we're still working on more items.'

It was not just the community who Derby were trying to keep fit; the players themselves were put on individual training regimes which involved three days of weights and a series of running requirements – all of which had to be fed back to the club at the end of the week.

When it came time for training to resume, Derby hosted a pair of behind-closed-doors friendly matches against Stoke City and also tested piping in crowd noise at Pride Park to see how the players felt and reacted to it.

Training was also intense to get players back up to speed. However, one player in particular needed quite a lot of fitness fine-tuning. Pictures surfaced of Rooney during the Millwall game with many commenting that he looked unfit for the resumption of football.

'To be fair, a few of the boys turned back up to training out of shape,' Lowe said. 'But yeah, I'd say Wayne wasn't fit enough to be starting games. Don't get me wrong, he could still ping balls all over the place. But he couldn't get about the pitch and that meant we had to carry his workload.

'I remember the first day back in training when we were allowed to play again – we did a 1,500m run. Which is like two laps of one of the pitches we would use for training. Wayne did one lap – basically walking the entire way – and then just went back inside.'

If Derby had not gone through enough personal strife, there was more bad news to follow. On 29 June Andre

Wisdom was stabbed in the head and buttocks trying to fend off four muggers who were trying to steal his watch at 4.30am. Wisdom had played the full 90 minutes against Reading two days prior and was returning to Liverpool to visit family. Although the injuries he sustained were not life-threatening and Wisdom was able to leave the hospital after a few days he would miss Derby's final seven games.

Wisdom was able to recover fully from the unprovoked assault and even spoke candidly about the incident with RamsTV, 'I remembered a lot of what happened, I was conscious through everything. I went into hospital, had a few operations, went home and recovered. In cases like that things happen really quick. I am a relaxed person anyway, so it is one of those things where you have to feel a sense of you have to be grateful that it didn't go another way.

'I had some wounds which I had the operation on, and the operation went well. From football's point of view it was more the mental side. The staff here have known me for a long time, they know what I am like, so I don't think that was a concern. I know myself what I am like, it wasn't that serious.'

Wisdom was well enough to attend the players' hotel prior to their 1-0 victory over Preston North End just a few days after the incident. His visit touched the players – and their response touched Wisdom himself.

'I don't get overwhelmed with emotion often, but that was one time where I had to talk to myself. I thought, "Could you cry here, maybe?" and then I thought, "No, definitely not, because the lads would be on to me for that." But that [seeing the players and staff] was nice. For me it was to show I am OK, and don't feel sorry for me, I am fine.'

Derby fans also stepped in to offer support for their stricken defender. They set up a GoFundMe page with the goal of raising £2,500 for a giant flag which would don the empty seats at Pride Park for the rest of the season. Supporters opened their hearts – and their wallets – to collectively donate £5,939 in total. The banner was purchased and the rest was given to charity.

Wisdom spoke out about the incident with *The Beautiful Game Podcast* in May 2023.

'I was at a place where I shouldn't have been. At a party,' he said. 'When I was leaving, about five guys with balaclavas and knives said, "Give me your watch." I said no. So we start fighting. I drove home after the incident. After I got home I realised I'd been stabbed multiple times.

'They ran off, I'm covered in blood in the street. I went home and then rang the ambulance from the house. I don't know how they [the media] knew. My phone was blowing up and I was thinking, "How do you know?"

'It was frustrating. I came out of hospital after two or three days and had a couple of operations, my body just wasn't the same. I tried to get back into football but it just wasn't the same. I wasn't getting the same output from my body in terms of power or speed. It's why to this day I haven't been playing. My left side has severe nerve damage. But my right side isn't as bad. I got stabbed in my head and started suffering from headaches. I couldn't breathe too well because I had fluid on my lungs. I think I rushed back to football. Once I could walk – which was about two weeks – I was coming back. I played two games but I knew I wasn't right. But in my brain – my contract was up too – and I was just playing so I could be in the shop window, and then rest in the summer. But then I tore my groin.'

Wisdom admitted that, mentally, he was almost desensitised to the violent nature of his incident due to his circumstances growing up, 'I think everybody has got traumas from different stuff. I come from a place where these things happened. You go to bed and hear gunshots. I've seen people stabbed, I've seen people fight until their heads have been busted open. The incident just made me more vigilant.

'I'd say the only way it really affected me was sleep. I couldn't fully settle. I'd always wake up a lot of time during the night.

'I remember at Derby they offered me therapy about what had happened, but I didn't really get much from it. I knew all of the things – feeling upset, sad, paranoid, anxious – but I wasn't. I just didn't feel it. I felt cool. Mentally I was OK.'

12

BLM, the Knee and Combatting Racial Injustice

MANY PEOPLE wish for football and politics to be kept separate. Others believe football has an active role to play in politics as demonstrated when sport has been used for political gain in the past, and some believe the two entities are intertwined making it impossible to separate.

Regardless of stance, one could not ignore how football decided to approach the Black Lives Matter protests and the death of George Floyd.

The peaceful protest had become a staple of the sporting world after Floyd's murder in Minneapolis, US, on 25 May 2020 when a police officer pressed their knee against his neck while he was on the ground for over eight minutes. Black Lives Matter protests were visible on a global scale and part of their repertoire was taking a knee. However, many believed the organisation were themselves racist, Marxist or just did not want politics so in their face in a football match and thus this was the crux of the discord.

Derby themselves joined the debate internally and gathered as a group to discuss if they would take a knee pre-match. Every player and member of staff joined in the meeting, as did Mel Morris who wanted to address his squad but many members of felt his message missed the mark – some felt it really rather insensitive with some of the things he said with one or two players visibly bemused.

'We thought he was taking the piss,' one squad source said. 'I'm not going to go into what he said – but I remember one of the boys nudging me and saying, "Is he for real?" It was really bizarre and I don't think he understood how what was happening impacted some of the black members of the squad.'

Nonetheless, Phillip Cocu, the club and the players felt it important to take a knee pre-game as a peaceful protest – Derby even covered it extensively in their matchday programme with some of the senior black members of the squad speaking up.

The protest was fine when games were being played behind closed doors – it was when fans attended again that the PFA, EFL and individual clubs started to sweat, fearing some of the reactions would sour games and even impact attendances, so much so that it felt like everybody was passing responsibility as to whose decision it was to take a knee.

The EFL said the issues were with the PFA, who themselves said the issue was with the EFL and the clubs – several clubs then reported that they were waiting for guidance from the EFL, with the EFL stating they had sent a memo to all clubs instructing them to take their own stance on the matter – a memo which Derby felt weak and absolved the governing body of any responsibility in the matter. Some sources at Derby also claimed that no memo ever reached their inbox.

Two instances made Derby think about their stance, along with several meetings. The first came at Millwall in December 2020 when a small number of people were back in the stadium during a brief period of some Covid restrictions being lifted. A large section of the Millwall supporters present booed relentlessly during the pre-match taking of the knee, which irked just about every player and coach on the touchline. Entering half-time at 0-0, the Derby squad held a quick players-only meeting between themselves, orchestrated by Colin Kazim-Richards, Duane Holmes and defender Andre Wisdom. The trio roused their team-mates by calling on them to go out in the second half and beat Millwall to silence the crowd. They did just that with a scruffy goal from Jason Knight but the fallout was also grizzly.

Wayne Rooney called the booing 'sad', while Millwall defender Mahlon Romeo had to be calmed down by club staff – which took about 15 minutes – before addressing the post-match media in which he accused the Lions fans of 'spreading hatred' while also highlighting the level of disrespect he felt personally.

He said, 'Today's game, to me now, has become irrelevant. The fans who have been let in today have personally disrespected not just me but the football club. What they've done is booed and condemned a peaceful gesture which was put in place to highlight, combat and stop any discriminatory behaviour and racism. That's it – that's all that gesture is.

'And the fans have chosen to boo that, which for the life of me I can't understand. It has offended me and everyone who works for this club – the players and the staff.'

Striker Kazim-Richards branded the reaction an 'absolute disgrace' on Twitter while Rooney said in his post-match interview that he would not condone the behaviour.

Kazim-Richards was one of the leaders when it came to how Derby moved forward on the issue and also represented an interesting contrast to many players. The Turkish international striker never took a knee, instead choosing to stand tall with his fist balled up in the air – he 'stands proud' as he said on Twitter and saw taking a knee as a submissive act, not one of power, adding: 'You will never see me kneel.'

The second instance was during a 1-1 draw with Nottingham Forest in February 2021. Kazim-Richards scored a thunderbolt which gave Derby a point in the game. Later that night, he was confronted with several messages from social media from Forest fans racially abusing him.

The matter was reported and the club moved swiftly to deal with it – but for Kazim-Richards it was the straw which broke the camel's back: 'I was on the phone to somebody from the club to let them know what happened. I thought my son was asleep. He comes in asking who called me a n****r and a monkey. I've had my son ask me why black people in movies are bad guys. I've told them it's acting and not real: don't take it seriously. It's like the conversation you have with your kids about sex. So I had to tell him that no matter in life, you will have some people who see you a certain way. But you are not a problem. Your skin, your hair, it's beautiful. A part of my children's innocence was taken by the perpetrators.'

Instead, after internal meetings and consulting with several black members of the squad including Kazim-Richards and Andre Wisdom, Derby decided that before each game they would vacate the pitch and stand on the touchline locking arms.

'It has been decided, as a collective group, to no longer take a knee. This decision has been made because the symbolic gesture of taking a knee is not enough; more needs to be done and we are committed to playing an important role in this,' read a club statement. 'Derby County is proud to continue its work with many fantastic organisations and individuals, both nationally and in the local community, to strive for equality and diversity in not just football but society.

'We will support the fight against all forms of discrimination by delivering the unified message of standing together as one. No longer taking a knee does not change the club's stance on all forms of discrimination. It will not be tolerated at Derby County; this is categorically clear.'

A key part of the decision for Rooney was not wanting to put across the image that Derby were divided in their stance. As well as Kazim-Richards, Wisdom had also started to stand during the pre-match knee and the visual created more debate than unity amid column inches and Twitter mentions.

Derby first displayed their new act of solidarity at home to Coventry City on 1 December and Rooney thought it made for a more striking sign of unity as opposed to taking a knee.

'For us, we obviously back it [taking a knee] as a club. No one wants to see racism in football or in any other walk of life. So we back that,' Rooney said ahead of the Coventry game. 'I only noticed in the last game that Andre [Wisdom] was standing up as well, where Colin [Kazim-Richards] is standing up, now Andre is not taking a knee. It is something I can speak to the players about but I think the league has to deal with it. I think there needs to be a message, and that message needs to be as one.

'I don't think it is right that some teams are kneeling and some teams aren't. There maybe needs to be a different message which everyone sticks together with.'

13

Cocu's Demise

THE ASSENT to Wayne Rooney's position as manager seemed far-fetched at one point, but when the 2020/21 season started to unravel it did so quickly, helping put the player in the frame to take the manager's position. The top-half finish achieved in Phillip Cocu's first campaign had sparked optimism, partly due to the late play-off push the Rams had mustered at the back half of 2021/22 – once football had returned from its three-month, Covid-induced hiatus – partly because now the players had a year in his system so were more used to playing his style, and partly because they now had Rooney for a full season.

The blueprint Cocu and Morris wanted to follow in 2020/21 came from an old enemy.

Leeds United travelled to Pride Park in July 2020 one day after having their automatic promotion to the Premier League confirmed following West Bromwich Albion's defeat to Huddersfield Town.

Many of their squad turned up to the East Midlands that day still red-eyed from celebrating the night before. They proceeded to outplay the Rams for 90 minutes on their way to a punishing 3-1 victory, which was the final nail in the coffin of Derby's play-off hopes.

Leeds pressed better, they ran more, they attacked with more purpose and verve – it was Derby who looked hungover.

After the game, Cocu noted Leeds had set the bar for where Derby aspired to be, 'Yeah [we lacked intensity today]. I made myself very clear at half-time and even at the drinks break. I thought the second half we came out much better and scored a good goal, but within two minutes they scored the equaliser and from that moment on Leeds were the better team, and more likely to win it, and that's exactly what happened.

'They're a good team. Physically they're the best team in the league – they run with so much high intensity. For us it is a hard lesson. We know what we have to improve on the physical part.'

Once the final-day victory at Birmingham City was out of the way the preparation for pre-season began in earnest ahead of 2020/21. There was a heightened expectancy over this particular pre-season due to the unconventional nature of the previous one – Frank Lampard had arranged, it, then shortly joined Chelsea, and Cocu met his squad several days after the start of it. However, due to Covid-19 restrictions, the 2020 friendlies would all be domestic.

The bid to get his Derby side up to par physically saw Cocu undertake a rugged pre-season filled with double sessions and lots of running. But with such a truncated campaign due to the fact the previous Championship season had only ended 28 days prior to the start of the Rams' first friendly against Peterborough United, some players questioned whether the intense physical style of training was necessary.

'We'd just played nine games in the space of about five weeks,' Duane Holmes said. 'And the start of the next season was maybe only six weeks away. We only got two weeks off. We didn't need the double sessions of running as well as pre-season games every three days. Some of the boys' legs were shot by the time we got to the season already. It was basically like we all had an international break between seasons so it didn't make sense to have all these intense drills.'

Some of Derby's new signings were far from impressing either. Again this was the transfer window with which most intrigue would be drawn from as Cocu was finally able to land more of 'his' players. In came winger Kamil Jóźwiak from Lech Poznań, centre-back Mike te Wierik from Groningen, plus full-back Nathan Byrne and goalkeeper David Marshall – both from Wigan Athletic – to help tighten up an often leaky and soft back line.

With Te Wierik in the fold, the writing seemed to be on the wall once more for Curtis Davies. The Dutchman was signed as a replacement for Davies and conversations were being held between Davies and Cocu about how to move the experienced former captain on. However, things quickly changed. In fact Te Wierik had played just three competitive games – defeats to Reading, Blackburn Rovers and Preston North End – before Cocu turned to Davies once again.

'I love Mike to bits,' Davies said. 'But he was really struggling to adapt to the English game. He struggled and got sent off against Preston in the cup, then really struggled when we got battered 4-0 by Blackburn and then Phillip brought me back into the side – almost seemed like trying to save face and I was a bit all over the place. Did he want me or not? Was I a last resort or not?'

Te Wierik would play only 93 more minutes for Derby after his subpar showing in the 4-0 home loss to Blackburn.

On top of all of that, the style which Cocu so desperately wanted to impress on his squad was not being very well received. Players found the system passive, with too many instructions and not enough individuality.

'From the only full season I was there for [2019/20], I can honestly say the football was not very enjoyable,' full-back Max Lowe remarked. 'We were such a passive team, passing slowly, never breaking the shape, and had to follow orders to a tee – Cocu was quite militant in terms of how he wanted to play, where he wanted his players to play and where he didn't want to see them on the pitch. It sucked some of the freedom from us. We also sat off teams too often. We'd press occasionally, but then we'd just sit back and hold our shape and let teams play around us.'

Not only was the football on the pitch slow, it mirrored what training had often become – long, drawn-out and predictable, yet extremely complex, and, in Cocu, the ideas were lacking a man who could put them across in practical terms.

'The sessions were slow,' Holmes said. 'And he'd do things like have us all wait around for two hours just to do a 25-minute passing drill in the afternoon. When you've got no responsibilities at home you can do that – but some of the older boys don't want to be waiting two hours between sessions, when they've got kids, just to do one thing that lasts less than half an hour.

'But I have to say that personally I enjoyed what he was trying to do technically. He was getting the best out of me, I was playing my best football of my career, I was getting back into the USA fold – he'd really turned my game around.'

Colin Kazim-Richards was also brought in on a one-year contract early in the new season, after Chris Martin departed following the two sides failing to reach an agreement on a fresh deal – something Cocu had openly pushed for in the media.

Martin and Cocu's relationship had not got off to the best start, but the manager's reliance on the striker and his natural fit within the Dutchman's system prompted a change of heart when it came to how important he was to Derby's plans, having contributed 13 goals and seven assists in 40 appearances in all competitions across 2019/20.

However, there were many bumps in the road when it came to negotiations. To start with, Martin was one of Derby's highest earners, and the heavy spending in previous years, the EFL charge in January 2020, the Covid-19 pandemic costing millions in revenue, and Martin's advancing years meant Derby did not want to make another hefty financial commitment to the player. Martin was offered a one-year contract that was heavy on incentives with a base salary which was below the average for a player of his age and position in the division.

The deal also featured an extension which the club could trigger should they wish – offering Martin little protection. He was after a minimum of a two-year contract to try and squeeze the most out of a playing career he knew was on the back nine. Derby offered Martin a contract on three separate occasions, each of them rejected.

Much of the same was true for midfielder Tom Huddlestone. He had been a mainstay in ten games of Cocu's tenure, starting and finishing each of the first nine. However, a torn hamstring while scoring a penalty against Barnsley in a 2-2 draw in October signalled what would eventually be the end of his career at Pride Park – he would play just one more league game, getting 90 minutes against Hull City during a 1-0 win in January 2020.

More to the point, Huddlestone felt disrespected at still remaining out of the squad upon returning to training in June to begin the resumption of football after the Covid-19 shut-down. Huddlestone had been working on cutting some weight to help him get about the pitch quicker and maintain strong fitness levels now he was well into his 30s. When a seemingly unfit Wayne Rooney was selected for the first game and the former Tottenham Hotspur player was left completely out of the squad, that was the final straw.

Derby did also offer Huddlestone a contract. But, like Martin's, it was heavy on incentives – ones he felt he was never going to get due to the fact he could no longer even make a matchday squad, let alone get on the field.

Kazim-Richards's introduction was initially a deflating one for Derby fans, many of whom believed it was a step backwards for the club. However, what the striker brought with him was more than just a presence on the field; he brought leadership and authority off it, too.

'The changing room was really quiet – we needed somebody like Colin in there because he's vocal. He's got a big voice and he's not afraid to use it,' a source close to the dressing room said. 'I told Phillip that we needed him for leadership if nothing else – somebody to get the boys going, make the changing room a lively place again because it was like a library.'

Of all the outgoings, Max Lowe and Jayden Bogle were let go for a fee, moving to Premier League side Sheffield United. The pair were two of Derby's brightest young players – but that also meant they were assets to sell as the club looked to navigate through choppy waters brought on by Covid as well as their own spending.

'I was going to sign my new contract that day,' Lowe remarked. 'It was a four-year contract, we'd been working for ages to get it over the line because at first Cocu didn't want to give me one that was so long, I wanted to make sure me and him were going to mesh well together before signing it – it was a long process.

'I'm driving to the training ground to sign it and my agent rings me and tells me not to sign it. I thought he was going to meet me there because he wanted to get in on the photo op or something. But he's telling me not to sign it because Derby have just accepted a bid for me from Sheffield United and things are moving quickly.'

Lowe and Bogle were present for Derby's 0-0 against Barrow in the League Cup first round, but neither were in the matchday squad and both sped off to Sheffield shortly after the full-time whistle had gone to discuss terms and complete their medicals.

Also departing – although not until January – and going back to FC Groningen, his former club, after just four Championship appearances, Te Wierik admitted he had not played well enough during his time at Pride Park. It was noticed by his team-mates.

'He just wasn't good enough,' Holmes said. 'You could never, ever fault his attitude. He always gave it his all, never heard him whining when he wasn't picked, and he was a top lad – but he just wasn't good enough. I think the pace of the division caught him off guard.'

Jordon Ibe and Bobby Duncan were also recruited (both on a free, though Fiorentina had a 20 per cent clause if Derby sold Duncan on) as very high-risk but high-reward options with the pair having checkered pasts – both would be popped into the under-23s while they gained fitness, but the hope was they could provide an attacking spark once up to speed. It never happened.

Ibe returned to the club after having a successful loan spell at Pride Park in the 2014/15 campaign when he was Liverpool's next bright young hope. Then an exciting 19-year-old, he was an electric winger, drawing similar comparisons to Raheem Sterling – his Liverpool team-mate at the time. Ibe's introductory interview after re-signing was a placid affair, talking of a 'new chapter' and being 'hungry' to play for the Rams.

Ibe played just three first-team minutes after re-signing, coming off the bench in an uneventful 0-0 draw against Stoke City in December 2020. He had impressed in the under-23s, scoring inside two minutes of his debut with a thunderous effort, but behind the scenes some players found it difficult to integrate Ibe into the group.

'He was a bit of a loner,' one source said. 'He's spoken about his mental health issues and depression, you want to try and help him. But it can be hard. He would cut himself out from the group and you'd never be sure how to approach him. He'd come into the canteen with his headphones on, music blaring, get his food and sit on his own. Sometimes he just wouldn't turn up to training, or flat-out refuse to do what the conditioning coaches were asking of him.'

After Ibe arrived, a member of Bournemouth's staff got in touch with Derby personnel to tell them that he was 'hands down' the worst player they'd ever worked with and not to touch him with a bargepole.

There was also difficulty training him. Ibe had stacked on muscle during his time away from football after being released by Bournemouth in June 2020, but Derby needed him to become a touch learner so he could burst away from defenders and have the stamina to go for a full 90 minutes. But getting him to do the running proved a challenge. Ibe would often argue with coaches and storm off into the changing rooms.

Ibe was also travelling back down south to London frequently and would often miss morning training sessions the day after. Some described the winger as a self-saboteur. During Wayne Rooney's time as manager, Ibe would occasionally put together a string of impressive training sessions which would lead to his selection – only for Ibe to then put in a poor session right before a match and then go missing leading to him falling further down the pecking.

Meanwhile, Duncan's only competitive chance came in the FA Cup third round against Chorley in January 2021, when the entire first team had to isolate due to Covid. As the season went on and the team's lack of goals continued to frustrate, there were calls from some fans to give Duncan a go at Championship level, but under Cocu he had never been fit and then did little to impress under Rooney.

Colin Kazim-Richards on the other hand was a much more successful signing, but he had to wait for his chance. The Turkish international was training in London and helping school kids with sport when he got a call from Derby to come and train with them. Kazim-Richards made his way to the club and put in a week of training on trial before looking to thrash out a deal.

Mel Morris, however, was less than keen to make it happen – or at least wanted to try and save some pennies on it. In the end, no agreement could be reached and the former Celtic striker went back down south until Cocu rang him and pleaded with him to return for one last training session. Kazim-Richards relented, put on a show at training and, together with Cocu, convinced Morris to hand out a one-year contract laced heavily on incentives such as goals, assists and appearances.

The deal took so long to complete, however, eventually being done in October, that Kazim-Richards would have to work his way into fitness and would not be fully at Cocu's disposal. In fact, under Cocu, he would play just 51 minutes of football – all from the bench – and failed to register any impact on games as he returned to fitness but also tried to find his place in a sinking team.

With the crammed-in pre-season finished and the bargain signings acquired, the 2020/21 season began. The Rams lost their first three, in worrying fashion, the first time that had happened to them in 28 years, including an abysmal 4-0 home defeat to Blackburn Rovers – which could have been 7-0 and nobody would have thought it was a harsh scoreline.

The performance also fuelled some resentment towards Rooney from some members of the squad. Rooney was dreadful at the base of midfield; his passes were often wayward, he left big holes for opposition runners to exploit and failed to close down quickly enough. He was not alone, however. But more was expected from him. Some highlighted his subpar showing in the defeat to Blackburn and felt his place in the starting XI should be questioned but it was also believed that dropping him was never going to happen such was Rooney's standing at the club.

After that game, Cocu lamented the performance and some of his own decisions in a match and aftermath which all but signalled he was on the edge, 'A big part of our defeat is about our attitude. Our passion, our willingness, our desire to defend, to track back, to close down the midfielders and not give them a free shot. It was too open. The defence runs back too deep and then gives the midfielders the space.

'You can talk about tactics – 4-3-3, 5-3-2 in the second half – it's part of the game. But in any system it's about how you execute. And when I see how they [Blackburn] play. I see the desire; they run, they go 100 per cent … I see it sometimes with us. Sometimes. But sometimes we don't deliver. To concede three goals in three minutes says it all.

'We played some good football in the first ten minutes. But what I'm worried about is how we present ourselves when we don't have the ball. We had 65 per cent of the ball. So they had 35 per cent – so what did we do when they had the ball? It's not good enough. It's unacceptable. I expected that we would have learned from bad defeats last season and our attitude.'

The defeats Cocu was harping back to were abysmal results and performances in the 2019/20 season to the likes of Brentford, Charlton, Fulham and Reading – all 3-0 away losses. After the first one, against Brentford before the first international break in September 2019, Cocu had accused his side of having a poor attitude and being arrogant, believing they were just going to turn up and play nice football and win. The clobbering against Blackburn had eerily similar vibes, which the former PSV Eindhoven manager noticed.

'I know that attitude is still there. Because you have certain characters, types of players – Jason Knight or [Graeme] Shinnie – I don't have to tell them,' Cocu explained, banging his hands together as a form of sign language for fighting, passion and commitment. 'But other players have to find it within themselves.'

A particularly eye-opening decision was Cocu's choice to put Matt Clarke, Derby's reigning player of the year, on the bench in favour of Te Wierik at centre-back. The Dutch defender would spend the next four matches on the bench and acquire a meagre 93 more minutes for the club. Clarke had been Derby's best defender since his arrival on loan from West Bromwich Albion and although he was working his way back to fitness and 'in rhythm' after returning for a second loan, his omission coupled with the hammering at home made for grim optics.

'After the game, it's hard to say that it was the best decision I made when you concede four goals of course,' said Cocu.

The cliff edge was crumbling under Cocu's feet. Reports swirled that he had one game to save his job or face the sack. The rumours were debunked, but nevertheless the chatter never ceased. And if Cocu did have one game to save his Derby tenure, the opponent was hardly ideal: high-flying Norwich City, fresh from being relegated back to the Championship but still armed with a plethora of attacking options.

Of course, with the speculation came counter-speculation and internally Derby strongly denied that Cocu's head was on the chopping block. The message from the top was simple – the start of the season hadn't been ideal but there were still over 40 games to go. However, the fact that just four matches into the campaign Cocu's job was seemingly under threat displayed an underlying tension between the manager and Mel Morris. But solidarity was the message ahead of the Norwich game. Cocu, Morris and Stephen Pearce were all pictured pitchside first in deep conversation and then having a chuckle together.

Somehow, through dogged determination, solidity, teamwork and a sprinkling of stardust courtesy of Rooney's 88th-minute free kick, Derby snatched a 1-0 win. Cocu clenched both fists in delight and tightly hugged Twan Scheepers and Rooney.

Some of the players remarked how Rooney believed he'd 'just saved his [Cocu's] job' with the goal – and there were few arguments about it with several players believing their manager would have gone had they secured anything but a victory.

The result bought Cocu seven more games as manager – but no further wins. More infuriating was the three-game period where Derby took a 1-0 lead in each of them, against Nottingham Forest, Queens Park Rangers and Bournemouth, only to be pegged back late on.

Throughout the final matches of his tenure, there were obvious cracks and hints that Cocu was now more a desperate manager trying to save his job rather than worrying about his philosophy. He changed from his classic 4-3-3 to a 3-4-3, which many of the squad enjoyed, found simpler to understand and also felt the team clicked better – and for the most part they did.

But as three consecutive 1-1 draws frustrated Cocu and inched him ever closer to the sack, he tried one last roll of the dice – by going back to 4-3-3 at home to Queens Park Rangers on 4 November. They lost 1-0 and were flat, lifeless and without attacking intent.

'I don't understand why he did it,' Duane Holmes remarked. 'We were playing well in the 3-4-3 – obviously not winning games but getting positive results and playing better – and I just think he was clutching at straws. You could feel and see he was under pressure and he was just desperate for another win.'

'He would always chop and change something. He was always changing his mind on what he wanted for each game,' Curtis Davies added. 'Especially at the back. You build up chemistry by playing together next to your centre-half. So when as a defender you're in and out of the team, or changing the system, it always held us back a bit.'

'He would try to bring me in for a Wycombe game because of how physical they were and to deal with direct balls – fair enough, it's tactical. But as a centre-half you need to develop a partnership by playing games together.'

The defeat would be Cocu's final appearance on the touchline but, technically, not his final game in charge. In the build-up to the home clash with Barnsley three days after the QPR defeat, Cocu, along with Morris and Pearce, was forced into isolation after coming into close contact with Pearce, who had tested positive for Covid-19. That left Liam Rosenior, Twan Scheepers and Chris van der Weerden in charge – with Van der Weerden in constant communication with Cocu over the phone.

'I've been at clubs before when you can tell the writing was on the wall and … this felt like it was that time,' Holmes said. 'At first I had to ask if Cocu really needed to isolate, or if it was a tactic to get him out of the spotlight – he was suffering and we could all see it. I would also say that he never lost the dressing room though. Usually that happens with a manager but I don't think Cocu ever did. He was always at the training ground working, trying to figure out a solution, trying to turn things around – and we could see how hard he was trying. But it just wasn't working. And I think the fact that Chris was his assistant – so technically in charge – but left everything to Rosenior said a lot about how his own staff felt about the situation too.'

If Cocu didn't lose the dressing room, behind the scenes he was annoying one member of his coaching staff – Liam Rosenior. Some believed Cocu saw Rosenior as a threat to his tenure, and his extensive knowledge of the

Championship – which he tried to pass on to Cocu – was often met with resistance, much to his young coach's annoyance. What further fractured the relationship, however, was the fact that Cocu, Scheepers and Van der Weerden would all speak in Dutch during coaching meetings and leave Rosenior looking puzzled. Other coaches would remark on how rude and disrespectful they felt it was but, like many things, Cocu would laugh it off.

Ironically, Rosenior would do most of the heavy lifting in training and team meetings, and would call the shots on the matchday itself when Cocu was isolating. In the build-up to the Barnsley game, however, he met further resistance from his two Dutch counterparts when trying to lead meetings. Open mocking of Rosenior's presentations and tactical meetings attempted to undercut any points Rosenior was trying to impart on the squad and it was a slog to just get a team prepared for the game with so much infighting going on between the coaches.

'That game was strange because it was almost like everybody jostling for power,' Curtis Davies said. 'Phillip wasn't there but technically his staff – Chris and Twan – were in charge effectively. But really nobody was put in charge and told "right, you're taking the role over". It was between Liam, Wayne and Justin – they put a team together. Which usually they would anyway as coaches. But because there was no head coach, it was a struggle for power. Because nobody knew their pecking order.

'You'd be getting info from one of the coaches, then another set of info from another. And it wasn't to say any of the info was bad, it just came across a bit like a coaching session in school. And not because they're bad coaches. It was because we couldn't put anybody in charge for that game. I think Liam was technically the head because he had his Pro Licence, but they hadn't announced it that way.'

The behind-the-scenes fighting and lack of unity was played out on the pitch. After a sluggish first half an hour in which Derby failed to establish any rhythm, consistency or even routine shape against Barnsley, things unravelled quickly when David Marshall's loose pass across his own box allowed Conor Chaplin to latch on to it and lash the ball into the net.

Rosenior 'panicked', in the words of Davies, and at half-time changed from a 3-4-3 to a 4-3-3 but to little avail. The defeat saw Derby fall to the bottom of the Championship and their form represented their worst start to a season since the dreaded 2007/08 Premier League campaign when they amassed a record-low 11 points. The only blessing was that the stadium was empty of fans due to Covid-19 restrictions, otherwise the boos would have been deafening, and Rosenior knew the club was not doing itself or the fans justice.

'I can't afford as a coach to make excuses about mistakes because this is 11 games now so I have to look at myself, everyone at the club needs to look at themselves,' he said after the defeat. 'This is a huge football club and we are not doing it justice. There's no way this club should be in the position it's in and I have to hold my hands up to that as well.'

That would be the end of Cocu and a week after the defeat he was relieved of his duties just 16 months into a four-year contract. Twan Scheepers and Chris van der

Weerden were also let go. Cruelly, Cocu still had a week of isolation to complete. He was not even afforded the opportunity to go and clear out his desk at Moor Farm. Although he could not see his players in person, he got in touch with each one of them by text message. He thanked them for their efforts under him, apologised for the way things had gone and wished them all the success in the future.

'When he was eventually sacked and able to come and get his stuff, he came in and said goodbye to everybody,' Davies added. 'I remember he pulled me to one side and told me that he knew I'd not had all the game time I'd wanted under him and said that, despite the fact he wanted to get rid of me at one point, that he respected my fight and wanting to stay and the determination. For me, even though our relationship on a personal level was OK with him, that made me really respect him more, and I took from it that he really respected me.'

Underpinning some of Cocu's demise was the presence of Rooney. Talk of Cocu not particularly wanting Rooney at the club and the signing being thrust upon him was doing the rounds amid the squad in earnest. Rooney had been brought in as a player-coach, but did little in the way of coaching outside of sitting in on video sessions and passing on some advice to several players.

'If he liked you, he'd offer you advice,' Max Lowe remarked. '[Max] Bird, [Jason] Knight – they were his boys. I think he saw some of himself in them. He liked them. Waggy [Martyn Waghorn], too. But for some of the lads it was a bit hard to integrate with Wayne. Obviously we were at a different level from where he'd come from.

I think it was hard to find a bit of common ground with him sometimes.'

Whispers had also spread through the squad that Rooney had a clause in his contract that he was going to be the next manager – something which created somewhat of an uneasy tension within the changing room.

'Sometimes you didn't feel like you were just playing with Wayne the player. You felt like it was an audition to see if the next manager wanted you there,' said Lowe.

'It was a bit strange. There was always this sense that Wayne was here to be the next manager as well as be our team-mate. So sometimes it could feel like you were playing for a place under him if and when he got the job.'

That was not a feeling reciprocated by all, however.

'I'd heard whispers that he had been gunning for the job while Cocu was still in charge. But I never found that to be the case,' Davies said. 'Wayne would go into the coaches' meetings and stuff, he'd sit in there watching videos. He was just a player that gave his opinion on how the team could be better. And give a pitch-level review. But he did have a big pull.'

The dynamic between Cocu and Rooney was awkward behind closed doors and would rear its head on more than one occasion, most famously when the player lost his cool following a 3-2 defeat away at Luton Town in January. Rooney admitted to losing his temper, but the extent of it was extraordinary.

'It was quite funny actually – but also a bit strange,' Lowe, who received the first red card of his career in that game, said. 'He [Rooney] came in and smashed a coffee machine on the floor. I was bricking it thinking he's going to come for me in a second. But he didn't. Phillip was about to speak but Wayne interrupted, and he went right after Matt Clarke and was calling him out, telling him his performance wasn't good enough. It went on for a bit and then Phillip tried to follow on from Wayne but it came across a bit … weak.

'Players do sometimes have something to say at full time obviously. But nearly always the manager ends strongly with a message that gets heard or just something that underlines the manager's authority. There was none of that there. It was a bit strange and I could see how it might undermine Phillip.'

Outside of the feelings of Cocu occasionally being undermined, the manager was not helping himself with some of the squad. Rooney was often the first name on the team sheet, usually in midfield, and the rest of the team was built out around him. Players believed that Cocu was not really in charge of whether Rooney played or didn't; moreover, some grew to resent the perceived special treatment he was given.

It was never made clear if they were designated days off or not, but Rooney would occasionally not be at training on a Monday.

'You'd come in on a Monday and we'd break out into our warm-ups and people would ask where Wayne was,' Lowe said. 'I think Waghorn would get a bit annoyed especially as he and Wayne would play on the PlayStation together and stuff – they were pretty close – then Wayne wouldn't show the next day.

'We never got told if it was a day off or if he was injured or excused for personal reasons. None of that. He just wasn't there. Then obviously he'd come straight into the team at the weekend and it meant guys like Duane, or Graeme [Shinnie], or Knight, or [Krystian] Bielik had to drop out of the team.'

Outside of the seemingly favourable squad selection, Cocu would also vent his frustrations at other players – even if Rooney had a poor game. It garnered resentment towards both Cocu and Rooney.

'When we got spanked against Blackburn at home, Cocu had a go at everybody – except Wayne,' Holmes said. 'Nobody played well that day. Not a single one of us. And Wayne was included in that. Why wasn't he dug out like the rest of us? I just didn't like it. But then again I felt for Phillip because it seemed like his hands were tied. I didn't honestly believe he was the one picking Rooney every week – he's a smart man, he could see he wasn't playing well at the time.

'I'll never have anything but nice things to say about Phillip and his staff. They looked after me when I lost my best friend and then broke my leg in the space of about three weeks and I was in a really bad mental space – they would always look out for me.'

14

Derventio Holdings (UK) Limited

AMID PHILLIP Cocu's spiral towards the sack, another bombshell was dropped on the club – it was revealed that a senior member of the Abu Dhabi royal family who failed with bids for Premier League powerhouses Liverpool and Newcastle United was interested in a Derby County takeover believed to be worth around £60m, which included acquiring the stadium Mel Morris had previously sold to himself.

Talks had been ongoing since May 2020 with Morris now actively pursuing a sale of the club – especially since Covid-19 had further drained his finances to keep Derby afloat. Although the message was always that Morris was not aggressively trying to sell up – instead claiming that it was merely investment he was looking for and would only sell to the right buyer – he nonetheless would engage in talks to sell the club to various parties, including Bin Zayed International (BZI). They were the first of many to be linked with purchasing the club.

The man in question on this occasion was Sheikh Khaled bin Zayed Al Nahyan – the cousin of Manchester City's owner Sheikh Mansour. However, as the process trundled along, even that relationship was questioned as several inside Derby discovered the two Sheikhs were not directly related as once thought – which therefore put any valuation on their wealth into question also. Sheikh Khaled owned the Bin Zayed Group, a Dubai-based conglomerate. In late September 2020, Derventio Holdings (UK) Limited was registered at Companies House, with three directors: Bin Zayed Group managing director Midhat Kamil Kidwai and two Swiss-based British entrepreneurs, Andrew Obolensky and Christopher Samuelson. Sheikh Khaled was listed as a 'person with significant control'.

The naming of the company Derventio was by no means a coincidence or a mistake. Derventio was a Roman town that grew to become the modern city of Derby. The talks had gathered such momentum that representatives of the company attended Derby's home defeat against Watford in mid-October.

The cat was now out of the bag, and on 6 November 2020 Derby released a statement confirming that not only were BZI attempting to buy the club, but that the proposal had passed the EFL's Owners' and Directors' Test and the transaction was 'expected to close very soon'.

The informal term for what followed among the fanbase would be 'scenes'. Fans changed their social media avatars to photoshopped pictures of Mel Morris wearing the traditional Arabic male headdresses and would decorate their social media handles with UAE flag emojis amid other signals that they fully approved of a takeover which stood to make the Rams one of the wealthiest clubs in the world.

On the other side of the coin, however, a very serious question beckoned – what of any potential human rights issues?

Or the potential for Derby County to become the latest brand to be involved with any sort of sportswashing? After all, a group being taken over by the cousin of Manchester City's owner, a club whose ownership has faced constant questions of such issues, wasn't something to simply brush under the carpet.

They were questions which, largely, didn't seem to bother many fans. A lot, after all, did just wish to enjoy the football and not have their fandom brought into a bigger debate about supporting regimes or being complicit in sportswashing or human rights abuses.

However, those fears were, for the most part, put to bed by Sheikh Khaled not having any active say in any policy-making in the UAE. He was royalty – but also an independent businessman using his own wealth to buy the club.

Fans were on a high on that November night dreaming of a January transfer window filled with signings. The next statement Morris and BZI would jointly put out, however, would not be until six weeks later and not to confirm any sale but instead to pour cold water over what they believed was speculation.

In mid-December, The Athletic reported that the takeover was in doubt after it emerged that Sheikh Khaled owed a law firm around £500,000 for work carried out during his failed Newcastle United takeover the previous year. The report was a bolt from the blue for fans. However, Pinsent Masons had obtained a High Court judgement against BZI on 9 September – a mere week after Derventio Holdings (UK) Limited was established.

The report angered higher-ups at Derby and BZI, who immediately set to work on a statement in a bid to wrestle back control of the situation:

'In order to remove any ongoing speculation, both parties want to assure Derby County's supporters that the acquisition of the club by Derventio Holdings is on track, with a view to completion before Christmas.'

BZI's failed takeovers of Newcastle and Liverpool put the EFL on alert immediately when the group emerged as buyers for Derby – particularly with the debt still owed to Pinsent Masons.

Christmas would be the second deadline BZI would miss and the knock-on impact would trickle down to the rest of the club. On Christmas Eve the *Daily Telegraph* reported that Derby were unable to pay their players and staff on time for the month of December, chalking it up to an unexpected delay in the takeover.

In a memo to the players, Stephen Pearce said:

'On behalf of Derby County Football Club, Mel Morris, and prospective new owners Derventio Holdings, we collectively apologise, that due to an unexpected and last-minute delay in the closing of the sale transaction, that your December pay will most likely be delayed until next week.

'We have been assured by Derventio that the closing funds have been remitted, but as at this morning they had not arrived in their lawyer's client account. As soon as they arrive, the transaction will close and we will process any outstanding payroll amounts immediately.'

The announcement also meant that the EFL officially placed Derby under a transfer embargo until they had paid their staff and players. The ruling came at a brutal time as Wayne Rooney was looking to strengthen his squad significantly before the window closed in an attempt to engineer a remarkable turnaround and save the club from relegation. By this time, Duane Holmes and Mike Te Wierik had already been sold – however, very little money was recouped, with Holmes going on a free transfer, which included a 20 per cent sell-on fee and was heavy on incentives – which could have reached as high as £200,000. Te Wierik, who was recruited as a free transfer, went back to FC Groningen for an undisclosed figure – which was again believed to be £0.

While players were understandably irritated by their late wage payments – some even expressing genuine concern at the latest development as they too had been assured that the completion of the takeover was simply a matter of days away, believing what they were being told by the club – they were more annoyed that, once again, they had been kept in the dark, as would become a trend throughout these takeovers and administration, on an issue which directly impacted their employment and, in this case, salary.

The players and staff waited, and waited, and waited further still but no money dropped into their bank account. A compromise was eventually reached, but not until late January – over two weeks after the date by which Pearce had said payment was 'most likely'. The club acquired extra funds – it was unclear from where, but a report another loan had been taken out by the club from MSD Holdings suggested that was the source, although Morris himself could have also covered costs – and with those funds the club had agreed to pay the players a flat rate. Derby felt it the best course of action. The flat rate enabled them to cover the entirety of some wages in the squad while acting as partial payment for others.

The board did have some trust restored in them, though, when the January wages were paid on time at the end of the month as expected. Some inside the club were annoyed that such a happening warranted a news story – but the fact that Derby had butchered the December wages meant the regular (or irregular) payment of wages warranted further inspection. It would not be the last time this happened at the club.

Meanwhile, another spinning plate was dangerously wobbling and looked to smash at any moment – the proposed BZI takeover.

A report in the *Daily Mail* revealed that Derby were beginning to make contingency plans for new owners as they became increasingly frustrated by the lack of progress in BZI closing out the deal as the talks entered late January – a full 74 days after the club and Derventio Holdings (UK) Limited released a joint statement declaring the deal would be closed soon. Erik Alonso was touted to be waiting in the wings with a bid of his own (more on that later) as was an American firm. Former owner Andy Appleby was also rumoured to be part of a consortium looking to put a bid together to take the club back. However, the American played down the suggestion and would only be interested in a takeover should the club absolutely need fresh ownership to save them from going out of business

– something which, at that time, he did not believe would happen. He would of course increase his interest when such a possibility was very real.

To add to the worrying news, Derby had taken out a second loan from MSD Holdings – the investment group which it was believed had ties to US billionaire Michael Dell. Morris had taken out a loan with the company in the summer of 2020 as he continued to chase fresh investment and had gone back to the well again. It was believed that Morris secured the loan against the training ground – meaning if things went pear-shaped and Derby defaulted on the loan, MSD could move in and take control of what would then become their asset – Moor Farm.

In his podcast *The Price of Football*, football finance expert Kieran Maguire explained why taking out the loans was such a dangerous ploy for Derby amid the takeover:

'If there is a takeover, most loans organised by specialist boutiques will have what's referred to as a change of control clause.

'Which could mean that A) they're entitled to their money back when a new owner comes in, or B) if they do a risk assessment [on] the new owner, it could be that there's an interest rate hike or the present owners of Derby County will have to pay some form of financial penalty.

'So, they're involved, they've been spoken about in terms of further funding and then there was another report, as a result of this, there is a potential for Derby County to go into administration. There is no way you want any club to be going into administration because that means two things: A) job losses, and B) some schmucks can be charging £300/£400 an hour for the privilege of being the administrator but it also would result in an automatic 12-point penalty.

'Given where Derby are in the league, it's bad news.'

By this point, worry was starting to consume the club. Stories followed of another loan, late wage payments, a transfer embargo and a takeover which now seemed more likely to fail than succeed and was now being held together by club statements trying to wrestle back control of the narrative.

While the players had their own concerns, they were kept so in the dark about how things were progressing that they almost had no choice but to believe the club.

'I, like most of the boys, I bet, was finding out everything on social media. Sometimes you would ask journalists if they knew of any updates because we weren't getting any,' Curtis Davies said. 'But even with all the reports of it going wrong – I never once thought Mel would let the club go bust or go into administration or anything. He's a fan and loves the club so I just always had hope that even if this takeover collapsed, another one would materialise and we'd be OK.'

Derby were going on the offensive when it came to controlling the message, with CEO Stephen Pearce appearing on BBC Radio Derby on 14 January 2021 to address the takeover. Pearce was bullish – perhaps taking notes from Morris – and said he'd had conversations with the players as to where they were with regards to the takeover, adding an assurance to fans that the deal was going to take place.

'The deal, from our perspective, we've heard nothing from either party – Mel [Morris], BZI or Derventio

Holdings – of any problems whatsoever with the takeover. As late as last night and this morning, we have been told that it absolutely is taking place,' he told presenter Chris Coles during his on-air interview. 'All of the legals and the documentation is completely done, it's just a case of that final closing of the deal now between BZI and Mel Morris.'

There was also a desperation in and out of Pride Park for a deal to be completed to save Derby from the spectre of administration – something which the club had insisted would never be a real possibility and was mostly scaremongering tactics from the media to whip up a frenzy. Pearce, in the same interview, assured supporters that the issue was more about timing than anything else:

'We're speaking daily to the prospective new owners, myself, Mel, and there's not been a single issue raised by either party. It's just all about timing.

'I assured the players yesterday that that is the case. It's an unfortunate situation that we're in but one that we see light at the end of the tunnel very soon.'

That interview and set of assurances bought Derby a bit more time when it came to appeasing the fans' ravenous appetite for change and the safety of their club. However, behind the scenes things continued to fall apart – the deal was always looking unlikely from Christmas when the players were paid late and it was said to be an issue with BZI transferring funds.

Finally, after almost a year of talks between BZI and Morris, and five months after the takeover chatter became public, the deal collapsed after BZI failed to meet yet another deadline to transfer funds – the third such deadline they had missed. Moreover, the Abu Dhabi-based consortium were still battling to settle their £500,000 legal bill following their failed Newcastle approach.

While the club had been projecting to the fans that the deal was always close to completion, it is believed that was simply trying to put a positive spin on things. While it is true that Derventio Holdings were approved by the EFL – what exactly they were approved for was not a full takeover. Various stages of approval must be met before a takeover can be completed. In reality, Derventio Holdings were never close to purchasing Derby County. The organisation had never produced any proof of funds they could buy the club or run it sustainably for at least a year.

15

The Curious Case of the Co-Managers

WITH PHILLIP Cocu's departure came the obvious question: who would take over? Liam Rosenior was the most qualified of the candidates having been one of the youngest coaches to obtain his UEFA Pro Licence. Wayne Rooney was in the middle of his coaching journey, with Covid-19 putting a stop to him doing his UEFA B badge, and also had the name value and plenty of high-profile match experience under him. Both had not made any secret of their desire to one day hold a top job.

There was also the ever-imminent takeover by Abu Dhabi-based consortium Derventio Holdings (UK) Limited, which would appoint a new permanent manager once the deal was completed – of course, it never would be. But the reasoning of sticking with just an interim until completion was sound enough – especially when names such as Rafa Benítez and Eddie Howe were being thrown around. The messaging being conveyed was that Derby were on the brink of becoming one of the richest clubs in the world and could attract any number of high-profile managers and players – any manager brought in during the immediate aftermath would be a stand-in regardless.

In fact, the takeover seemed so legit that Rosenior revealed that all the coaching staff had met with the new potential owners.

'We all had a Zoom call yesterday,' Rosenior said ahead of Derby's clash against Bristol City in November 2020. 'Myself, Wayne, the coaching staff, Stephen Pearce and Midhat. I can't say new ownership yet because it's not fully done. But it was just to put a face to a name and I think it went really well.'

The solution in the short term was to have Rosenior and Rooney be co-managers with coaches Shay Given and Justin Walker assisting them, and Steve McClaren overseeing the whole operation in a quasi-coach role. Both Rooney and Rosenior very openly wanted to be managers – and specifically Derby manager now there was an opening – and the squad recognised it too with a 'soft power struggle' being felt among the players. Mentally, there were two camps – team Rooney and team Rosenior.

'I think once the manager had gone, Wayne was really up for taking the job,' Curtis Davies assessed. 'He saw an opportunity to manage a very good club, a good way in. They brought him in as a player-coach anyway, so they had some reason to bring him in that way. Maybe Mel did say that one day they would make him the manager.'

The temporary setup was odd, but Mel Morris believed it could work. He felt that each coach brought a certain set of skills to the table and, if used properly in collaboration, could bring success in the short term. Morris also never ruled out the option of permanently instating Rooney and

Rosenior as co-managers. What Rooney lacked in formal coaching he more than made up for with the wealth of knowledge and exposure he'd had to top-level coaches. Rooney often stated that Dutchman Louis van Gaal was the best manager he worked under in terms of details and tactical input into games. Rooney would also point to Sir Alex Ferguson's man-management at times, but of course the pair's relationship became more complex over the years. Rooney didn't divulge how much exactly he leaned into Ferguson's way of management – but his actions during his time in charge of Derby suggested he had learned quite a lot from his old boss. Rooney had also spent the previous ten months learning from Cocu and his staff as well as having a more hands-on role in the coaching – it was nothing major at first, simply joining the meetings and watching video clips as they prepared for the next opposition. Rooney would also have a small input into how he saw the team on the field given he was playing each week and could get more of a feel for things from on the pitch.

As for the more formal elements of coaching, that would be left to Rosenior. He was already familiar with putting on full sessions and was even given the task of leading some sessions under Cocu – though not many. The former Brighton & Hove Albion defender was at home with a whistle around his neck and a stopwatch in his hand. During the co-manager arrangement, Rosenior would be laying out and putting on most of the sessions while Rooney would remain an active part of the squad. Rosenior was a much more hands-on coach than Cocu, electing to muck in with the squad and try to teach them by way of doing, not telling – Cocu so often having done the latter, and getting frustrated when the orders were still not followed. Both Rooney and Rosenior wanted to try and instil a more relaxed vibe around the camp and part of that was joining in with things and encouraging rather than condemning.

Justin Walker was also assisting, and the club higher-ups felt his link to the academy players – having spent a couple of years as the academy head coach – was vital in getting the best out of a young group. With Max Bird, Jason Knight, Louie Sibley, Lee Buchanan and more now-established members of the first team, and with further youngsters expected to make up the squad, Morris wanted a bridge from the academy to the senior team on the coaching staff.

Shay Given, who'd been the club's goalkeeper coach the season before, was now a senior coach on the staff and would not only assist with the goalkeepers but would have a say when it came to set pieces. Given's expertise at corners was especially effective. Derby would roll out a series of routines which would have the opposition bamboozled in their own penalty area while the Rams often had a man free, sometimes two. Or somebody to tap in a scruffy knock-down. The chaos would start around the penalty area with Derby players lined up in a row – similar to what England did in the 2018 World Cup – before each member of the squad would sprint to their assigned spot in the penalty area. Of course, at each corner the pack was shuffled and players would line up the same way but then different players would spring to different spots causing even more confusion. Derby would score

THE CURIOUS CASE OF THE CO-MANAGERS

four goals and create untold panic for weeks on end until teams finally figured out how to stop them; Given was a valuable resource.

The first press conference with Rooney and Rosenior as co-managers was unusual. There they both sat next to each other on the Zoom call ahead of Derby's away clash against Bristol City like key characters in a hilarious buddy cop film as a flock of national and local journalists populated the online meeting space. The oddity wasn't just that Rooney and Rosenior were fielding questions on the recent departure of Cocu, the newfound arrangement and how things would play out – it was that nearly nobody cared about Rosenior. Every question initially asked was directed at Rooney – did he want the job? Would he still be playing? Would he be selecting himself? That one got some disingenuous laughter from the 'room'. What kind of manager Rooney saw himself as was also posed. Then, almost to just make Rosenior feel part of it, he would be asked to tag along for the answers at the end of each interaction. The 44-minute press conference was a slog with both men putting forward their answers to questions, and journalists wanting to know everything from how close the takeover was to if Rooney was a tracksuit or suit manager to if Rosenior felt he was in the running for the job.

For all the internal optimism that the dynamic managerial duo could provide a spark for Derby and get them back on the right track, it wasn't to be. The experiment lasted two matches. An attritional, lifeless 1-0 defeat at Bristol City was followed up by a miserable 3-0 battering at the hands of Middlesbrough at the Riverside

Stadium. Rooney played in midfield for both games, acting as the manager on the pitch while Rosenior barked orders and encouragement from the touchline. Derby were rigid and lacked any real vision outside of two banks of four in an attempt to make them hard to break down – it worked in patches, but it was not enough. The system also sucked any creative life out of the team and left them tossing crosses or long balls into the box in the hope that Martyn Waghorn, Colin Kazim-Richards or some other helpless chaser could get a lucky bounce of the ball and make something happen.

The defeat to Middlesbrough marked Rooney's final game as a professional footballer as he was soon named sole manager and officially retired from the game. In a meeting with Steve McClaren, Rooney, Rosenior, Walker and Given were all told of the plan to scrap the co-manager arrangement and hand the decisions over to Rooney. Some disputed that meeting ever took place, instead insisting that the decision was taken between the four coaching staff and they agreed and felt one voice was best – and Rooney was best to lead that and be that voice. However, it is at odds with the fact that both Rooney and Rosenior were applying for the job on their own merits. Would Rosenior really defer to Rooney of his own will? It was, naturally, rather tough to remain in lockstep while also presenting two totally separate ideas for the club moving forward in their own right. That is not to say Rooney and Rosenior did not present good ideas – but the power struggle and the battle of egos to get ideas across created a confusing atmosphere.

During the hiring process, Rosenior delivered a slick presentation with his credentials, methodology for moving the club forward and his identity of football. The presentation impressed Morris and Pearce – as well as some of the BZI group who were among the listeners, at a time when that takeover was expected to be completed. Rooney also gave his managerial pitch with tactical framework, a list of transfer targets he wished to acquire and also played into his high-level experience at Manchester United and working under some of the game's greats – Morris felt that some of that managerial wisdom from Sir Alex Ferguson, José Mourinho, Louis van Gaal, Fabio Capello, among others, would have soaked into Rooney's brain and he could lean on that, while using Steve McClaren's assistance, to build the basis of a solid manager.

There were persistent rumblings that Rooney had been promised to be the next manager of Derby as part of his terms of signing. It was a rumour which seemed equally plausible and improbable – why would Morris sign Cocu to a lucrative four-year contract only to promise Rooney the manager's job in two years' time and thus committing to paying Cocu compensation to the tune of half of his contract? Why would Morris commit to Rooney who, while his knowledge of the game could never be questioned, lacked formal coaching badges and any level of managerial experience? And while all parties involved in the deal denied that was ever an official, or unofficial, term, the rumour refused to go away and it was felt by the players, which threatened to undermine Cocu even more so.

'He [Rooney] was after the job the moment Cocu went,' a source close to the dressing room said. 'There's nothing wrong with that. He'd never hidden the fact he wanted to be a manager. Liam was the same as well. They were both going for it aggressively but trying to work in harmony. It didn't work – but that also isn't their fault. It's the situation they were put in.'

Rosenior was also angling for the job in his own way.

'He was like a dog let off its lead and left to run around the park,' Davies said. 'Once Cocu left he just felt free, I think.'

'Suddenly Cocu left and Liam was so much more authoritative,' one former player said. 'On the one hand you wondered where that kind of energy was when Cocu was here. But then we didn't know what went off in the coaches' meetings and stuff. Maybe he just felt he could be himself more.'

Even though Rooney and Rosenior were doing their best to work in combination, the players also thought the setup was odd. Many believed there were too many mixed messages in terms of what shape was being played, how high the lines should be pushed up when on the field, or if they should play predominantly out wide or through the middle when building attacks. Even personnel decisions were a muddle. Rosenior and Rooney had loyalties to different players; for example, while Rooney was a big fan of Kazim-Richards, Rosenior bristled against the big striker – so how was the decision made as to who started? In the end, it was one of compromise – even begrudging compromise at times. As much as the public message was one of collaboration, internally the experiment wasn't working and it was time for one voice.

16

Rooney the Manager

USUALLY, A pre-match press conference for bottom-of-the-table Derby hosting fellow strugglers Wycombe Wanderers is not cause for anything of any note. But the 40-minute Q&A was worthy of plenty of media attention due to the fact it would be Wayne Rooney's first presser as sole manager.

'For the two previous games, the four of us [himself, Liam Rosenior, Shay Given and Justin Walker] were coming together and picking the team,' Rooney said. 'We felt that it needed one voice, one person to do that and make the decisions on the team and on the subs coming into the game – and we felt I was the right man for that. It's obviously exciting for me to do that. Management is something I've stressed I've wanted to go into.'

Although Rooney would be in charge, he would use Steve McClaren's experience as a manager while cutting his teeth in the role, adding:

'I'm confident in my ability to do this job, but Steve brings a lot of experience and knowledge to us. There will be times when I need to lean on Steve and get advice. I'm not naive enough to believe I know everything in this role so Steve will be very helpful to myself and the other coaches.'

Rooney's first match in sole charge was a nondescript 1-1 draw at home to Wycombe which also saw Colin Kazim-Richards score his first goal for the club. The experienced striker would go on to become somewhat of a talisman for Rooney's team.

Rooney talked about simplifying training for the players as their confidence was not in a place where they could take on complex tactical orders. It was a case of being solid at the back, being tough to break down as a team, playing the ball wide, being more direct and getting crosses into the box.

'After he got the job solo, he had a meeting with all the players and told us what had happened, how he was excited for the chance to be managing us and that every player can come to him with anything,' midfielder Duane Holmes said. 'He told us all that just because he's the manager he won't change – and to be fair to him, he didn't. He always stuck to his word about staying true to himself. He never let the power of being a manager change him.'

Under Rooney's guidance the Rams took ten points from their next six games, including wins against Millwall away and Swansea City at home – the former of which was marred by ugly scenes at the New Den when members of the home support booed the players taking a knee prior to the match. This was during the short period where Covid restrictions were lifted to allow small numbers of supporters inside stadiums.

As well as making the team more difficult to beat on the field, Rooney lifted morale off it too. During his early days as manager he often talked about seeing smiles on players' faces again and the mood in general being lighter. He could often not resist getting involved in training, something Phillip Cocu seldom did, which helped create a more relaxed vibe in sessions and he even moved the pre-match press conferences forward by half an hour so he could dash off and play head tennis with some of the squad.

But Rooney was not all smiles and games. After all, he had worked under some of the most ruthless managers of his era. And he had a ruthless streak in him, too.

Rooney immediately set about culling the squad of players he did not feel fit his squad, either on the pitch or in personality. One of his most public falling outs was with Duane Holmes.

The pair got on well when Rooney was still a player and had no personal ill will against each other, but a clash of personality came when he became manager.

'I played with Duane, and it's different when you become the manager, you have to make decisions, you have to be ruthless with your decisions,' Rooney said prior to the closing of the January transfer window in 2021. 'I like Duane as a person, he is a good bubbly character, and he didn't fit into my plans. I want the players working every day on the training pitch, that is important. If you don't do that, and I spoke to every player and explained if you don't put the work in, I don't want you at this football club.

'Unfortunately for Duane he fell into that category, which is a shame because he has got fantastic ability and he is a player I possibly could have used in the last few games but I am true to my word, if you don't put the work in then I don't want you.'

Holmes was irritated by the comments as he read them on Twitter and was unaware that his manager would be so public in his reasons as to why he was on his way out of the club. When Holmes went to clear out his locker at Derby's training ground before sealing a move back to Huddersfield, he found that his stuff had already been placed in a black bin bag and neither Rooney nor then assistant manager Liam Rosenior found him to say their goodbyes; instead Holmes waited around to find them both.

The public barbs seemed one-sided and painted Holmes as an unfortunate victim. But Holmes himself would almost justify Rooney's words and actions when giving an interview with Huddersfield upon re-signing for the club.

'A couple of months ago Derby played Huddersfield Town in a behind-closed-doors game and I didn't have to play, but I wanted to play because I wanted to come here and kind of drop it in to Leigh Bromby [Huddersfield's head of football operations] that I wanted to come back,' he said at his introductory interview on Huddersfield's YouTube channel. 'So, I played in that game and I spoke to Leigh and since then we've been working to try and get it done.

'I really got on with Wayne, I think he is a great man and a great guy. He's a fantastic footballer and I am sure he will be a great manager. Sometimes things just don't work out.

'I think it was clear for a while that we were going to be going in different directions and when the chance came to come back to Huddersfield I couldn't wait to get started and come back.'

Holmes received much criticism for the interview and many Derby fans pointed to it as proving Rooney's point in the midfielder not buying into the club any more and wanting out. But Holmes declared that those behind the scenes knew what really went on and that everything was not as it seemed.

'First of all – I've no problems with Wayne at all,' Holmes said. 'The narrative that we didn't like each other or that we'd fallen out just isn't true. We fell out over football matters – and that happens all the time in football. Nothing personal. We just had different ideas.

'Those comments I'd made when joining Huddersfield seemed naive to fans, or felt like I'd snaked them – but I did that because both me and Derby knew the situation well before I was having them chats with Huddersfield. Derby were happy for me to leave, Huddersfield were happy to have me, I was happy to go back to Huddersfield. It wasn't a case of trying to get the move first then tell Derby I wanted out – Derby wanted me out.'

The move might have happened a lot sooner as Holmes had spent the previous week training with the Terriers but all parties had to discuss and agree terms, and it is believed that he also had to negotiate his wage packet due to deferrals still not being fully paid up.

Jack Marriott was also quickly ushered out of the door. Early in the season the former Peterborough man was sent out on loan to Sheffield Wednesday but found himself back at Moor Farm to rehab a calf injury.

Derby had a recall clause in the loan deal and there was some mulling over of exercising it as Rooney had been desperate to add a striker to his squad in the January window. Ultimately, Derby signed Lee Gregory from Stoke City and Marriott was sent back to Yorkshire, but the decision to do so was not made until the afternoon the clause expired and Marriott was left somewhat annoyed by the timing of it all.

Rooney spent his January deadline day bringing in five new loan signings to bolster the squad as they fought to stave off relegation. The club had little to no money to spend on reinforcements so stop gaps would have to do. In came Gregory, winger Patrick Roberts from Manchester City, defenders Teden Mengi and George Edmundson from Manchester United and Rangers respectively and Beni Baningime from Everton. Rooney had a particular plan for Mengi, however, with the central defender a target for the summer also and the manager wanting to get the youngster acclimatised to his style of play and work before getting him for a full season in 2021/22 – of course a lot of that hinged on Derby staying up, of which Rooney maintained ultimate confidence over.

When Derby's form began to crater at the end of the season, Rooney took the squad to Wales a couple of days earlier than scheduled before a match with Swansea in May so the team could get a break, gel with one another, and hold each other accountable in a more friendly environment. There are arguments that the trip came too late in the day with only two games left in the season, and at first glance that would seem to be the case as Derby lost 2-1 to Steve Cooper's side despite going ahead through Tom Lawrence.

The ruthless side Rooney flashed during the transfer window was not reserved purely for outgoing players; some remaining within the camp felt it over the course of his managerial tenure, none more so than Martyn Waghorn and Festy Ebosele. Waghorn was dropped for a 1-0 away defeat to Stoke City in March, just days after Rooney had praised the striker's attitude in training. After the game, Rooney said that Waghorn's application to training on the Thursday prior had been excellent, but when he trained on Friday his behaviour 'wasn't acceptable', according to the manager.

The crux of the issue came when, entering Friday's session, Waghorn was asked to stand in for Colin Kazim-Richards, who had been carrying a hip injury, upon which Waghorn learned that he would not be starting against Stoke. The former Rangers striker did not take the news well considering that Kazim-Richards was in considerable pain. Waghorn assumed he would be starting. When that was not the case his application to training dropped in the eyes of his manager. Rooney and Waghorn got on well. When Rooney was a player rather than the manager, the pair formed a close bond, would often play on the PlayStation together and would support each other if they had any struggles away from the pitch – both had been open about their mental health challenges in the past and bonded over the subject. However, when Rooney took over as manager, he made it clear that their relationship would have to change – the ticking-off and omission from the Stoke game was such an instance of him laying down the law. Waghorn would be restored to the starting XI for the next match, a 2-0 home victory over Luton Town, and would lay on an assist before going off at half-time with an injury, but he would restore Rooney's faith fully with arguably his best performance in a Derby shirt when he scored two and assisted another in the tension-riddled 3-3 draw with Sheffield Wednesday.

In the case of Ebosele, the Irish defender was clearly talented but 'walked the line' more than once according to those with close knowledge of him at academy level, to such a degree that conversations were had about whether to release the youngster.

Rooney brought him into the first-team group, mostly out of necessity for cover for regular right-back Nathan Byrne. Ebosele played just 25 minutes – all from the bench – across three games at the back end of the 2020/21 season, but it was enough to convince Rooney to keep Ebosele as part of the group going forwards. So rocky was Ebosele's standing at the club that just three weeks prior to the dramatic 3-3 draw against Sheffield Wednesday which kept Derby up at the expense of their opponents, Ebosele was the closest yet to being released.

In March 2022, Ebosele, having featured regularly in the Championship season, agreed a five-year contract with Serie A side Udinese after rejecting a fresh Derby deal. The perceived lack of loyalty irritated some of the Derby higher-ups and coaches. Ebosele knew how at risk his career at Derby had been over the last 12 months and was seeking further security at a club, which the long contract offered, as well as a sizeable pay rise. Part of Ebosele also felt that some people at Derby had little faith in him. He was looking for a fresh show of faith, again rubber-stamped by the size of the contract on offer. However, in the weeks that followed, his commitment to Derby was in question and he was relegated back to the under-23s.

'Festy's attitude wasn't right, wasn't great. I left him out of the squad because of it,' Rooney said in April after Derby were relegated to League One following a 1-0 defeat to QPR. 'I know he's moved on to a new club but if you are here, you give it everything; Luke Plange [who had in January signed for Crystal Palace on a permanent transfer but been loaned back to the Rams for the rest of the season] is an example, who has done the same but he gives everything.

'The way I work, if you are off it, you can't play, you will not play whether we are fighting relegation, fighting for trophies, you won't play.'

17

The Final Day

AFTER THE defeat at Swansea City – a sixth successive loss – everything hinged on the final day of the 2020/21 season. Derby would guarantee their survival with a victory over Sheffield Wednesday, who themselves were fighting to avoid the drop. They would go down with a defeat. A point would be enough to keep the Rams up if Rotherham United, the other team challenging for survival, were denied a win against Cardiff City.

Prior to the match Wayne Rooney was calm. He told the waiting media that he planned to watch *Sister Act 2*, his favourite film, the night before the game and wanted to convey his calmness to his players.

Curtis Davies, who had torn his Achilles in December, was not medically cleared to play against Wednesday and signed a waiver so he could be named as a substitute. He spoke about the magnitude of the fixture, 'The only other time that was similar was when I was at Birmingham City, and we went into the last day of that season [2010/11]. But I didn't have the emotion attached to that day like I did to this one.

'There was a lot riding on this game for Derby. My emotions were highly charged before the game. But I didn't really show it because I was trying to lead other people. But I was highly aware that if we don't get a result here, we're going down. And players would move on – but the staff at the club might be out of a job. That was the reality of it. That was in my head. Then you're sitting on the bench and hearing Rotherham have gone 1-0 up, then we score and we're staying up and all the permutations. It was all a bit much on that last day.

'I'm focused because I have to be for the other players. If I'm a mess and all jittery – when I'm not even on the pitch – then that could rub off on the players. My focus is on what was happening on the pitch. Inside I was all over the shop. The crazy thing is, going on to the pitch made it easy. Whatever emotions I had – they fell by the wayside once I was on the pitch, because I was in a situation where I was in control. I was in a position where I could help. Those few minutes I was on the pitch flew by, but the previous 80 or so minutes felt like two days.

'I found Sheffield Wednesday's approach really strange. When they went 1-0 up, I don't believe they can sit on the game and try to see it out. But then they get themselves back to 3-2 up, and yet still left themselves wide open for Kamil Jóźwiak to make that run and get the penalty. Obviously I was delighted. But their approach made no sense to me. They should have shut up shop. And then even after it was 3-3, I didn't feel like they threatened us. It felt like a very tame effort at trying to win the game. I was ready to get beat up. Balls were coming into the box but I felt there was no real desire from them to get on the end of things. I don't know if in their heads they were spent and had nothing left and psychologically wilted away.

'It was definitely a situation that I never thought, during my time at Derby, that we'd be in. The side I signed for when I came to the club was a side that was pushing for promotion. We managed to do that the first two seasons, and then even under Phillip Cocu, even though it looks like we had a bad season, we got 64 points and were pushing for the play-offs in the final run in.

'The form we were in heading into that final day [one win in 13 matches], we should consider ourselves lucky that the season wasn't a little bit longer because the form Wycombe were in at the end [five wins from their last ten entering the final day] might have seen them overtake us.'

Prior to the game, Derby fans – still not allowed to attend fixtures under the existing Covid restrictions – marched to outside of Pride Park armed with banners, plenty of shirts and scarves and chants ranging from those about Rooney to ones aimed at Mel Morris to sell up – it was safe to say he was no longer welcome at a club which he called his own.

An early spanner was thrown in the works when Rotherham took an eighth-minute lead at Cardiff, immediately putting Derby into the bottom three. Further misery came when just before half-time Wednesday went in front at Pride Park, moving themselves above the Rams too. Derby were staring relegation full in the face but managed to find something from somewhere to not only draw level through Martyn Waghorn four minutes into the second half, but take the lead thanks to Patrick Roberts's sweet strike three minutes later.

The game was a rollercoaster, flinging Derby fans and players one way and then the other before coming to a screeching halt to climb another peak and then plunging them into a deeper valley. Callum Paterson levelled for the visitors just after the hour, before Julian Borner put Wednesday 3-2 up with 20 minutes to play, the two goals seeing Derby drop back down to third-bottom and second-bottom respectively

Matches of such magnitude are always tense, and this one was made weirdly even more so by the fact it was played behind closed doors. Every shout, scream, involuntary noise and demand could be heard. There were no chants, no shots of supporters in the stand looking on edge, just the raw drama of football.

Rotherham's clash with Cardiff was slightly ahead due to the amount of first-half injury time played at Pride Park, further adding to the twists and turns. Right as Kamil Jóźwiak was brought down for a penalty in the 78th minute, Cardiff had found a leveller against Rotherham in the 88th minute in the Welsh capital – but the Rams didn't know that.

Waghorn rolled up his socks, took a big puff of the cheeks and thundered the ball into the back of the net to cap his best-ever Derby performance in what would be his final-ever Derby game.

Not long after the equaliser, Davies came off the bench and completed his remarkable, not medically approved, return to give his all for the final eight minutes while Derby clung to their Championship status. He threw his head and body in front of every ball in the near vicinity of him.

At full time emotions ran wild. Several players were close to tears – some were in them – of joy of course. Colin Kazim-Richards spent a solitary moment sitting on the advertising hoardings, head down, soaking in the moment.

Rooney cut an emotional figure in the media room. Red-faced, head bowed in exhaustion, there was a slight quiver in his voice as he softly conveyed what the result meant to the club.

'I feel relieved. A crazy game. That game is the story of our season – up, down, good, bad. The important thing was we stayed in the division,' he said. 'When we went 3-2 down I thought the lads showed great character, great commitment to keep pushing and get that equaliser. We got it and then I had a decision to make with Curtis – do I bring another defender on and hope Cardiff don't concede? Or do I bring an attacker on and try to win the game? I felt the right decision was to bring Curtis on. We knew we had a bit of time left in our game due to a delay – so if we had to change it and go for a goal, I could do it with the personnel on the pitch.

'I knew they [Rotherham] were 1-0 up early in their game. And then we go a goal down. So I knew we were down if it stayed like that. My message at half-time was to stay calm, there's 45 minutes left. Don't panic. I brought Max Bird on to get some calmness on the ball. Then to go 2-1 up so quickly, and then concede again – a set piece. We did an hour on set-piece training here at the stadium yesterday and didn't concede a goal once. It's frustrating because the preparation the players are getting is excellent.'

Rooney quickly pivoted his attention to off-field matters. He had only been in the job for six months and had lived through one phantom takeover already before being sold the dream of Spanish businessman Erik Alonso and his consortium taking over the club and heavily investing to try and propel Derby into the Champions League within a decade.

The off-field matters had provided more than a hint of distraction for Derby and everybody connected to the club. Rooney himself consistently repeated to the media that the updates he was receiving from Morris and those engaging in talks was that the deal would be done 'imminently' – that famous word – and the club would be in safe hands soon. But imminently never came, and wouldn't come until more than 12 months later.

The manager said, 'I'm delighted for the players because this season, on the pitch, off the pitch, has been crazy. We need to sort it out quickly. What's going on? We need to move forward tonight. I've got plans in place and I need to move quickly on them plans. We cannot afford to have another season like we've just had. It's impossible for this club to allow ourselves to be in this position. If we move forward, I'm very confident in my ability to help get this club back to where it belongs.'

Outside the stadium, the party was in full force. Waghorn, Bird, Jason Knight and several others cracked open a beer and partied with the fans – relief and joy rolled into one. Kazim-Richards was encouraged to start the bounce – a regular occurrence, showcasing the relationship between the squad and the supporters – on his way to his car and duly obliged, which sent the fans into further frenzy. There was a genuine sense of feel-good around a club which had experienced so much doom and gloom over the previous nine months.

Rooney, however, was already turning his focus to the following season. He had circled several positions in the squad which he felt needed strengthening, the main one being a new striker. Colin Kazim-Richards had carried most of the load for the season and his form had earned him a fresh deal heading into the next year, but Rooney was keen to have the Turkish frontman play a less vital role in 2021/22 and wanted someone in front of him in the pecking order.

18

Take(over) Two: Erik Alonso

THE SORTING out of things that Wayne Rooney alluded to was the change in ownership. Rooney was hopeful of a buyer coming in but he'd seen false dawns before. After the takeover from Derventio Holdings fell through, Mel Morris pivoted swiftly to find a new custodian. It was now no secret that the Derby businessman was aggressively flogging the club amid its financial woes. Not only was Morris becoming increasingly frustrated at having to keep providing funding, losing millions a month and seeing no end to it in sight, his health was also starting to become a major issue. Morris had caught Covid during the pandemic and was also battling other more serious health concerns which required hospital care. The running of a football club required the kind of energy he was rapidly losing.

A wildcard surfaced in the shape of Spanish businessman Erik Alonso, who had previously been connected to Sheffield Wednesday and had failed in his attempt to purchase the Yorkshire outfit and continued to hunt for a football club to add to his portfolio, which he claimed already consisted of hotels and villas, a winery and mines.

Talks went slowly, Alonso claiming that Morris was difficult to negotiate with throughout most of the process. However, it was that toughness which Alonso respected as he claimed it was what made Morris so successful.

Alonso was bold, one might even say brash, most of the time. And his verbal – and sometimes written-to-Twitter manifesto – sounded tantalising. Alonso would secure all of the club's debt to himself ensuring that Derby County could be debt-free and he would ensure the stadium and the rest of the club's assets were put under one umbrella as opposed to being owned – albeit by Morris under two different guises – by separate entities.

Alonso was so confident that he went on an early PR and charm offensive, giving interviews to TalkSport and BBC Radio Derby, discussing his ambitions for the Rams including wanting to take them into the Champions League within the next ten years. It was the first of many red flags as fans thought the young businessman was overconfident and emotional – perhaps all the hallmarks they associated with Morris. But Alonso also had someone of real credibility behind him – former Real Madrid president and lawyer Ramón Calderón was advising him on the deal.

Alonso was even starting to get his hands dirty, speaking with Rooney on three or four occasions about his plans for when he was the eventual owner. He name-dropped former Chelsea sporting director Michael Emenalo as someone he had been targeting to get in and head up Derby's recruitment.

He also bandied about plenty of exciting names to bulk the squad up with, including Uruguayan playmaker Gastón Pereiro and attacking midfielder Gabriel Boschilia.

Alonso felt comfortable making such bold claims, however. A breakthrough seemed to be close when on 7 April a joint statement was released by Derby and No Limits Sports, the agency that Alonso ran, confirming an agreement had been reached for the sale of the club.

Yet the EFL had further questions and found the answers Alonso had provided to their questions already unsatisfactory. Alonso later claimed that the EFL constantly changed the criteria after he had submitted relevant documents – which included bank statements as well as a deposit of 40 million euros.

The EFL constantly asked for Alonso to provide evidence of the source of his money, but he was unable to do so to their satisfaction. There was even a claim that the money would be coming in from Luxembourg, which Alonso strongly denied.

Alonso even hinted that an unnamed American group would be the face of the project while he himself worked in the background, although the EFL insisted that the details of such a group were never disclosed to them at any point during the negotiations.

'There were three conversations with the EFL,' Alonso told The Athletic in June 2021. 'The first one was for proof of funds and to justify the movement between the banks. It had to be €75m over a three-month period. We would have meetings every Thursday. Initially, the EFL said it was OK, but they wanted to know the source of the funds. I said no problem, I provided all the information about the businesses and sent it to the organisation.

'Then they [EFL] came back and told me it was not sufficient. They asked me to provide all information for all business dealings I may have in Indonesia and Spain, including tax returns and bills. I then provided all that information. I spoke to my lawyers and they told me what we had provided was already sufficient.

'All the money was coming from my Spanish account. If I get profit from my company in Dubai or in Spain, it doesn't matter. All the money passed the money laundering checks in the Spanish national bank. All the money was coming from Spain.'

Alonso had even shown The Athletic bank statements that there was at least £35m in the accounts in Spain which were ready to be transferred over to UK accounts to begin funding Derby. However, that's where the legitimacy of the funds came into question.

The business dealings he had in Indonesia were another red flag which had inconclusive evidence one way or the other. Links had surfaced between Alonso and Indonesian businessman and politician Tommy Suharto, who had been sentenced to 15 years in prison after he was found guilty of ordering a hitman to kill a supreme court judge.

Alonso, who lived in Indonesia for eight years, never denied knowing Suharto and claimed that at no stage was he ever involved with the funding to buy Derby. Yet it was that sourcing of the funds, as well as the sufficiency, which ultimately meant the deal was never going to get off the ground no matter how much of a big game Alonso talked.

EFL chief executive Trevor Birch was strong enough to go on the record during an interview with TalkSport to declare that Alonso 'wasn't able to deliver' when it came to 'tangible proof' of funds.

Further question marks appeared over Alonso's political beliefs. It had emerged that his name had appeared in connection to the right-wing Spanish party Vox. Alonso had previously denied his affiliation with the party even though several of his social media accounts showed he liked posts from various Vox handles on Facebook and Twitter. Alonso simply claimed he knew many people in political circles and that following or liking posts does not equal an endorsement of them.

As the red flags continued to pop up and the takeover looked to be going the way of the previous BZI approach, the final nail came in a hilariously grim fashion. Alonso's Twitter account posted a video of an opulent all-white living room with the caption 'good morning'. It was in response to yet another request from the EFL to provide proof of funds. However, the post did not remain up for long. Fans quickly caught on to the likelihood that the video had been stolen from a TikTok handle which shows off fancy houses. It shot any remaining credibility Alonso had and he quickly deleted his Twitter account then claimed it was hacked and that police were looking into the matter.

Six weeks after the joint statement was made between Derby and No Limits Sports, the deal was called off. In reality it was never close as Alonso had not only failed to provide any proof of funds, he had also failed to provide a sustainable business plan, and clarity when it came to the sourcing of the funds. Alonso had often made comments about an American businessman – whom he claimed he refused to name for legal reasons – and claimed they would be partners, thus debunking the rumour that the mystery partner would be a front for the takeover and Alonso would be pulling the strings from behind the scenes. There was just one problem with that plan – at no stage during the process was the EFL ever alerted to the idea of an American consortium being involved with the deal and Alonso failed to provide any names, businesses or any evidence at all of this party.

It was no surprise that the Alonso deal collapsed having never truly got off the ground to begin with.

19

A New Dawn?

WITH NO takeover in sight and the prospect of administration becoming a clearer reality, Wayne Rooney, his staff and whatever players he had available to him set to work for 2021/22.

The previous season Rooney often admitted that he did not have the players or time to implement his way of playing and instead had to adapt to what personnel he did have and to the situation the club found themselves in with trying to keep their heads above water. As a result, Derby played very direct football, working the ball from back to front quickly, with longer passes and often working it out wide to get a bombardment of crosses into the box for Colin Kazim-Richards, Lee Gregory, Martyn Waghorn and others to attack.

Really, Rooney wanted to play front-foot football with an emphasis on playing out from the back, but not in a passive way which had besotted so much of Phillip Cocu's tenure. Tempo would be the key factor and having the bravery to play risky passes. However, the squad was still largely threadbare and the promised takeovers never materialised, leaving Rooney with an unbalanced, largely extremely youthful group which – as he admitted during pre-season – would struggle to be competitive if the Championship season was to start in July.

Nevertheless, Rooney and his staff set about implementing their philosophy with a much more hands-on approach than they were previously allowed when the high-stakes relegation battle demanded a match every three days, allowing for very little time on the training ground. It was about tight, sharp passing drills, dribbling drills which challenged players to be brave and take players on, and exercises designed to get more bodies into the box during attacks.

Ahead of their pre-season training camp, Rooney named Tom Lawrence as club captain, taking the role previously held by Curtis Davies. The decision was a surprising one for some – including Davies, but he held no ill will at not getting the armband. However, some of the players felt that there were more natural leaders in the squad with Graeme Shinnie, Davies, Craig Forsyth and Kazim-Richards all names some felt were ahead in the pecking order.

'Tom had a few injuries last year and was out for a long time, but when he came back, he showed a great attitude, determination and character to help us stay in the division,' Rooney told the club's website after announcing the decision. 'Tom is at an age and a period in his career now where he needs to step up. I believe giving him the armband will see him take on the responsibility and make sure he and the team do the right things.

'He has matured on and off the pitch and I think it is the right time, but we have a number of other natural leaders in the squad as well.'

The feeling that not everybody backed Lawrence as captain bothered Rooney somewhat – to such a degree what when an article in The Athletic was published about the subject, Rooney had the piece printed and asked the squad if any of them had a problem with the way he was doing things and requested them to stop leaking things to the media.

The move represented the final part of Lawrence's redemption following the drink-driving incident – with which Rooney may have sympathised with, having made mistakes of his own, including drink-driving.

'It's business as usual. I'm never going to change the way I am. I always welcome the lads and if they need to chat, I'm always there, and on the pitch I'm going to be demanding,' Lawrence said ahead of the 2021/22 season. 'It's massive for me personally and my family. But I'm not going to change too much and be dramatic over it. That's not who I am. If something needs to be said, I'll say it, if somebody needs shouting at, I'll do it. But I'm not going to shout just for the sake of shouting just because I'm captain.'

Some had reservations over the selection, however, believing Lawrence to only call out younger players and leave more of the senior players to their own devices when it came to criticism. Some also felt a leader should not have such a reckless accident such as the drink-driving incident on their CV – how could one take leadership from somebody who made such a bad decision?

Next on the docket was replenishing the depleted squad. For many players, such as Martyn Waghorn, the 3-3 thrilling climax against Sheffield Wednesday would be their final Derby match as their contracts expired.

Leaving the club were Jordon Ibe, Scott Malone, Jack Marriott, Andre Wisdom and Florian Jozefzoon, while loan signings Matt Clarke, Lee Gregory, Patrick Roberts, Teden Mengi, George Edmundson and Beni Baningime also departed.

Mengi was a particular frustration. Plans had long been for Derby to bring back the defender, and initially he was keen to return to Pride Park to get a full season of games under his belt and establish himself as a first-choice player in the hope of breaking through into the Manchester United first team upon his return.

Mengi was battling with injury which meant the club wanted to wait until he was fit again before taking him on, but there also seemed to be a lack of movement in getting terms agreed verbally. Rooney had done as much as he could to convince the player to come back, but the two clubs themselves could not agree terms. Eventually, Mengi stayed at United before going out on loan to Birmingham City in January 2022.

Rooney highlighted that several players he had been targeting for 2021/22 had already moved on to new clubs – he did not mention all the names, but it was believed that Manchester United midfielder James Garner, fresh from a loan spell at Nottingham Forest, was high on his list, and as many as seven players he told the club he wanted had moved already, causing a massive source of frustration for the manager.

The EFL had placed a transfer embargo on the club which would not be lifted until Derby had refiled their accounts for 2016, 2017 and 2018. Derby appealed the decision but in the meantime they could only register nine senior players for the start of pre-season. Throughout pre-season Rooney was using non-contract players – namely Davies, Phil Jagielka, Richard Stearman, Sam Baldock, Ravel Morrison and Sone Aluko. All but Aluko – who would sign for Ipswich – eventually stayed on once the club were allowed to sign players. However, Jagielka and Baldock would be let go in January when other clubs came in for their services and EFL restrictions meant the Rams were unable to extend their short-term contracts.

The restrictions for a club in dire need of warm bodies in the squad were tight. Derby were allowed to offer contracts of up to 12 months or a six-month loan deal if they did not have 23 players of a 'professional standing' – the definition of which was a single first-team appearance in a competitive game outside of the EFL Trophy. However, Derby did meet that threshold due to their FA Cup third-round tie against Chorley in January 2021 when they were forced to play a team of academy players after a Covid-19 outbreak forced the entire senior squad to isolate.

The recruitment drive did eventually start, and on a shoestring budget, with players who would first come in as trialists for Derby's pre-season games. As well as the non-contract players staying on and signing full terms, goalkeeper Ryan Allsop came in. However, the academy would be supplementing the rest of the squad.

Right-back-turned-winger Festy Ebosele – who later had difficult patches in the first team and even had Rooney question his attitude – was brought into the senior setup, as was winger Malcolm Ebiowei who quickly became a fan favourite for his agility, close control and ability to generally excite all of Pride Park, having signed in the summer following his release by Rangers. Luke Plange wouldn't see his competitive debut until December 2021, but Rooney had kept close tabs on him since the club snapped him up in March of that year after Arsenal had released him. Former West Ham midfield prospect Louie Watson would also be called on from time to time, as would three academy graduates – holding midfielder Liam Thompson, striker Jack Stretton and centre-back Eiran Cashin.

But in pre-season, all was looking bleak. After a 2-1 defeat to Salford City on 24 July, Rooney joked that, at the current rate, he would not be able to field a squad to compete in the first Championship game against Huddersfield Town.

Although the situation around the club was perilous, Rooney remained in good spirits. After the Salford match he stopped in the car park to greet waiting fans who all flocked towards him and he was patient enough to sign some autographs. He exchanged words with a couple of his coaching staff as to where they were heading after the game for a meeting and then he casually drove away. That, really, was that for the rest of the day. Yet what would unfold days later would be strange and slightly embarrassing.

Days later, photos emerged of Rooney drunk and passed out in a hotel room while three women – allegedly Snapchat models – partied, drank and took photos of him, including one 'mooning' him.

Rooney was, understandably, angry and contacted the police. The fear was he had been the victim of a setup. In the following days at Moor Farm, he explained the situation to the squad and coaching staff, apologised for any embarrassment caused and apologised to the club.

Phillip Cocu on the touchline during his first competitive match in charge of Derby County against Huddersfield Town in August 2019.

Phillip Cocu (left) and Wayne Rooney shake hands at Rooney's Derby County unveiling in August 2019.

Tom Lawrence (right) scored the first goal of the Phillip Cocu era as Derby County beat Huddersfield Town 2-1 in August 2019.

Former Derby County captain Richard Keogh was sacked after a September drink-driving incident in which he was a passenger.

Tom Lawrence (far left) and Mason Bennett (far right) leave Derby Magistrates' Court, where they avoided prison after admitting to drink-driving and fleeing the scene after September's crash.

Phillip Cocu (left) celebrates at full time after an emotional 3-2 win over Birmingham City at Pride Park in September 2019 following the drink-driving incident.

Wayne Rooney in action on his debut for Derby County against Barnsley in January 2020.

Players around the country began taking a knee pre-match in the wake of George Floyd's death in May 2020.

Chris Martin (far left) celebrates his 97th-minute equaliser against Nottingham Forest in an empty Pride Park as Derby continue their play-off push behind closed doors due to the Covid-19 pandemic.

Phillip Cocu (left) speaks with Mel Morris (right) and Stephen Pearce (centre) before Derby's 1-0 home defeat to Watford in October 2020, sinking Derby to just one win in the opening five games of the 2020/21 season.

Phillip Cocu was sacked by Derby on 14 November after 16 months in charge. Wayne Rooney and Liam Rosenior were installed as interim co-managers.

Rooney (left) celebrates with Jason Knight (centre) and Matt Clarke (right) following a 1-0 win over Millwall at The Den, Rooney's first win as a manager, which was marred by many fans booing when players took a knee pre-match.

Andre Wisdom sprints away in celebration after scoring a 94th-minute winner against Wycombe Wanderers in February 2021 as Derby battled relegation.

Colin Kazim-Richards celebrates a long-range goal in a 1-1 draw against Nottingham Forest in February 2021. The striker would sadly receive racially abusive messages the day after the match.

A mixture of relief and delight as Derby staff embrace following confirmation of their Championship status after a 3-3 draw against Sheffield Wednesday.

Jubilation for Martyn Waghorn, who scored two vital goals, at the full-time whistle following Derby's 3-3 draw with Sheffield Wednesday which ensured Derby retained their Championship status.

Captain Tom Lawrence scored two goals as Derby produced a shock 3-2 victory over Bournemouth as the Rams tried to battle relegation once again following a 21-point deduction from the EFL.

Chris Kirchner was in attendance in November 2021 as the American tried to buy Derby. The deal eventually collapsed due to Kirchner's inability to provide proof of funds to the EFL.

Derby fans marched in their thousands to Pride Park prior to their match against Birmingham City as part of the Save Derby County campaign, and to voice their displeasure with the ownership and the EFL.

Derby sold out Pride Park for the 2-2 draw against Birmingham, which saw Krystian Bielik score a 96th-minute equaliser with a stunning overhead kick.

Dejected Derby players (from left to right) Nathan Byrne, Ravel Morrison, Lee Buchanan and Louie Sibley applaud the travelling away support after a 1-0 defeat to Queens Park Rangers which confirmed Derby's relegation to League One.

David Clowes completed his takeover of Derby County on 1 July 2022.

Liam Rosenior was hired as interim manager following the Clowes takeover. Rosenior won seven out of 12 games in all competitions as manager, but was relieved of his duties on 21 September 2022.

Paul Warne was hired as Rosenior's replacement and led Derby to the cusp of the play-offs, but they fell just short after losing their final game of the season to Sheffield Wednesday.

The club also released a statement:

'Wayne Rooney informed the club yesterday that the pictures had emerged and that they had been taken without his knowledge or approval. After taking counsel the matter was reported to Greater Manchester Police who are currently investigating the incident. While that remains the case, there will be no further comment.'

There was a mixed reaction to the incident. Some believed it showed a lack of leadership and immaturity, while others sympathised that his privacy was breached and he had done nothing illegal – even if it had been silly – and, crucially, how Rooney spent his private time had nothing to do with them.

Nevertheless, with that out of the way, Derby set about getting their Championship season under way against a Huddersfield side which by season's end would be contesting the play-off final. Derby's starting XI looked strong on paper – Davies and Stearman formed a no-nonsense centre-back partnership with the steady Forsyth at left-back and the outstanding Nathan Byrne at right-back. Graeme Shinnie partnered Max Bird in central midfield, a pairing which often offered great balance as the pair complemented each other. The front four offered plenty of excitement in theory – but the personnel could also be hit and miss. Kamil Jóźwiak and Tom Lawrence on either flank could provide trickery and burst – but could also frustrate with the lack of a final product, and Louie Watson was still so raw that he was learning on the fly. Trying to get service from that trio was Colin Kazim-Richards – who had ended the previous season battling against injuries but was looking to pick up from where he left off – a campaign so successful for him personally that it netted him a new contract on better terms than his original one.

The problem was not necessarily the strongest starting XI, it was the depth of the squad. Morrison would help things in the attacking midfield areas but, for the 1-1 draw against the Terriers, Derby had six academy players on their bench. Even without a hefty points deduction hanging over them, there would be a mountain to climb if they were to avoid relegation for the second time in as many seasons.

The early signs were positive, however. Through their first eight games Derby grabbed ten points – including credible wins against Hull City and Stoke City – but it was always with the belief that the club was simply building up a buffer for when the inevitable happened.

20

Administration

ON 22 September 2021, Derby County officially entered administration. It was a prospect which many inside the club felt was inevitable. Mel Morris had been searching for a new owner for the club and several takeovers had come and gone. The club's finances were in a state with money owed to HMRC, but the timing of the announcement floored just about everybody with questions being asked about why it was done when it was.

The done thing in such a situation would have been to have placed the club into administration before 2021/22 got under way – thus putting all of the cards on the table. One would assume if the club started the season not being in administration then there was a plan in which Derby could see it to completion and had the funds to do so. It prompted more theories that Morris was either running out of money, or patience, or both.

The Rams had made a positive start to the season, collecting ten points from their first eight league matches – part of the drive to collect points in a hurry was to mitigate any deduction which may come their way.

The EFL docked them 12 points for falling into administration, leaving the Rams on minus two and dropping them to the bottom of the Championship table.

Morris, who said the decision to place the club in administration was 'gut-wrenching', continued to drive home lost revenue in the Covid-19 pandemic, saying it had cost the club around £20m. In total, Morris estimated that the club had lost him 'in excess of £200 million' to date.

He appeared on BBC Radio Derby in the aftermath to apologise and explain the decision.

'It's tragic, there's no question. I can only apologise to the people there,' Morris said. 'Am I disappointed? Yes. Am I sorry to the fans? Yes. I desperately wanted to get this club right up there if we could do that.

'From my perspective, I've put a lot of blood, sweat and tears – and a heck of a lot of money – into this club and it's had some really good times under my tenure, but ultimately I've failed.'

The courts set about appointing the administrators and settled on Andrew Hosking, Carl Jackson and Andrew Andronikou, all of whom were managing directors at business advisory firm Quantuma.

'We are in the early stages of assessing the options available to the club and would invite any interested parties to come forward,' said Hosking in a statement. 'Our immediate objectives are to ensure the club completes all its fixtures in the Championship this season and finding interested parties to safeguard the club and its employees.'

The decision sent shockwaves throughout football and became a point of contention as to whether the EFL should have final say over appointing administrators – such was the mess and frustrations with Quantuma.

Quantuma started as the salvage operation, but by the end fans almost wanted salvaging from the firm such were the missteps. They had been hired to oversee Bolton Wanderers' administration back in 2019 and, by all accounts, they were unimpressive in their role.

The club became such a state that people that experienced administrators in football believed Derby's situation to be one of the worst of any club to go into administration.

The EFL were left furious with Quantuma's work also – including the vetting of American businessman Chris Kirchner, who proved to never have the funds to run the club, blamed Queen Elizabeth II's Platinum Jubilee in June 2022 and subsequent bank holiday for the reason as to why he was unable to move his money, having earlier declared that he would be the next owner of Derby County, while the EFL had not seen his proof of funds.

As the time spent in administration increased and the club slipped closer to going out of business, the EFL began to panic – their biggest fear was that Derby County, just three years on from appearing in a Championship play-off final, were going to go extinct.

Derby owed HMRC in excess of £20m. They also owed American firm MSD Holdings around £15m as part of a loan taken out and secured against the training ground, and there was a sizeable loan from a consortium led by Swiss financier Henry Gabay too. To add to that, Derby still owed money on transfers, including outstanding payments to Arsenal for Krystian Bielik, and around £2.5m to Lech Poznań for Polish winger Kamil Jóźwiak. Jóźwiak had joined Derby in the summer of 2020 for around £3.4m, but Derby had only paid 25 per cent of the fee by the time they were placed into administration. In January, Quantuma had asked Poznań to defer the next instalment, which was due in February 2022, but the request was rejected. After that, Poznań claimed they had no further communication from Derby's administrators.

Furthermore, Derby had shipped players in January to raise funds to stay afloat. Graeme Shinnie was sold to Wigan, and Luke Plange, who had only come into the team in December 2021, was sold to Crystal Palace for around £1m but loaned back until the end of the season. Dylan Williams, the promising left-back, had moved on to Chelsea while David Marshall, who was no longer featuring under Wayne Rooney, was also removed from the wage budget and signed for Queens Park Rangers. As well as those outgoings, some of the players who signed on a free in the summer had their contracts expire as Phil Jagielka and Sam Baldock moved to pastures new. One final sale came in March when Kamil Jóźwiak moved to MLS side Charlotte FC.

The outgoings left the squad threadbare amid a relegation dogfight and Rooney had to lean even heavier into the academy prospects.

On a more human level, members of Derby's staff were fearing for their jobs behind the scenes. Staff would be made aware of club announcements at the same time as everybody else – usually seeing it through social media, which promoted anger and more fear. It trickled down to the players as well.

'I was more worried for the staff than us boys,' Curtis Davies said. 'Our contracts were protected by the PFA, and, horror of horrors, the club went under, we all had the security net of being able to find another club – now we might not be on the money we were, we might have to move, we might have to make some sacrifices of our own but our position was better than that of the staff. If you're there sweeping floors, making tea, cooking the meals and on whatever it is an hour – you need that to support yourself and your family. It was horrible. Some of the senior players were trying to get answers so we could relay it to everybody, but it was so hard.

'I'm not saying I or any other of the senior lads should have been part of the conversations regarding the long-term future of the club, but I feel everything could have been communicated better than it was.'

Staff were critical of the club's hierarchy for not being 'more up front' and communicating exactly what was happening.

Not helping matters was the lack of clear communication from Quantuma, who sent several mixed messages to various parties, which only served to further muddy the waters. Their handling of Derby left many fans confused as to what exactly they were being paid to do, and how they were going about achieving finding new owners for the club, and whichever member of the Quantuma team spoken to by fan groups, consultants and journalists would dictate the level of communication as well as the message being conveyed. In all, the court-appointed administrators left a lot to be desired and had rattled more cages than they should have done so early in the process.

21

The Kirchner Takeover

AS QUANTUMA searched for a new owner, the fans became increasingly concerned. Each passing day brought a news cycle filled with more questions than answers as Derby County got to grips with what administration meant for its short- and long-term health – if there was to even be a club at all.

A month after the club announced the decision, American businessman Chris Kirchner announced his decision to bid for the club. At the time the 34-year-old was the founder, owner and chief executive of Slync.io, a global logistics technology provider. He announced his intentions through a letter which was posted by the Press Association:

'We don't know each other yet, but we have two things in common: our love for the game of football and our desire to rebuild Derby County back into the proud club everyone deserves.

'My name is Chris Kirchner and I hope to see many of you soon – as this is my official announcement of my intention to work with the administrators to take Derby County Football Club out of administration.

'Derby County is a club with a rich history and one of the best groups of supporters in all of England.

'While the club is currently going through a really tough time, it is the supporters, and everyone associated with the club that have stayed loyal which provide the foundation to rebuild again.

'I want to be a part of that rebuild and support that effort. As an entrepreneur I am committed to building companies and I want to apply that experience towards rebuilding this proud and storied club.'

Kirchner then went on the PR charm offensive. He would take to Twitter to regularly interact with fans, sign off posts with the ram emoji and outline his plans for the club. It was seemingly a smart move for a man who understood the fanbase had often had to contend with sometimes conflicting reports of what was going on and craved more communication from inside the club. Supporters bought in. Many welcomed him with open arms to Pride Park – the man who would save Derby County and restore their battered club.

Kirchner courted the club and its fans not only with his Twitter account and rocking up to games in Derby apparel like he was already officially on the books – he would invite club personnel to golf events, offer fans his phone number and have a chat with them. He was schmoozing at a rate not even seen by Erik Alonso.

While reports continued to swirl around Derby's short and long-term future alongside reports of how the club was managing in the interim, Kirchner kept fans happy with communication continuing through his social media channels. However, that would change. After Kirchner made a bid for Derby in December and then upped the offer a week prior to Christmas, the deal began to unravel. Kirchner butted heads with Quantuma and on Christmas Eve 2021 he withdrew his bid for Derby County and instead turned his attention to another Championship side, Preston North End.

'It is with real sadness that I can confirm I am withdrawing from the process to buy Derby County Football Club,' Kirchner announced via Twitter. 'First and foremost, I would like to apologise to the fans. As you know, I've been in talks with the administrators for about two months.

'Two weeks ago, I made a formal offer to buy the club. I believe I presented a very detailed, generous and ambitious long-term sustainable business plan. It included purchasing the stadium, future funding and maintaining the academy's status. We improved that offer further today [Thursday].

'I wanted to agree a deal that I thought was in the best interests of all parties but, unfortunately, the last 24 hours has proven that just isn't possible. So it is with deep regret that I must now stand aside and let the administrators pursue their own course.'

Quantuma hit back with a statement of their own which read, 'The issues we are having to deal with are complex and we simply were not in a position to accept Mr Kirchner's bid as it did not meet the level of other bids received ... Whilst yesterday was a difficult time, it provided a stimulus to one of the remaining bidders who increased his offer for the club. We expect to name preferred bidder status imminently. We repeat that we are moving as quickly as possible to achieve a sale of the club.'

The process behind the scenes was difficult. Several parties who dealt with Quantuma testified to the administrators not being in lockstep with one another, saying they would even clash with each other such was the differing personalities of Andrew Hosking, Carl Jackson and Andrew Andronikou. Some described Hosking as quiet, tough to get hold of but perhaps the most sensible and approachable of the bunch. Jackson was described as the most aloof of the trio, often making stylish statements with little substance behind them, while Andronikou could be rather confrontational if pushed on questions – sometimes even towards fans. It was this cocktail which made them tough to deal with for Kirchner, while Quantuma were never satisfied that Kirchner had the funds to run the club once it was in his possession.

The truth was closer to Quantuma's statement than Kirchner's. The deal was complex; Quantuma not only had to find somebody to buy the club, but a debt repayment scheme with HMRC also needed to be hammered out at 25p in the pound or the club was at risk of going into liquidation and the EFL, behind the scenes, were preparing all alternatives to avoid going down a route which would lead to Derby County not existing.

Kirchner's background was also troubling to the EFL. A man whose company was a startup being bankrolled by Goldman Sachs – an investment banking group which the EFL had much experience with when it came to potential buyers being set up by them – whose entire business worth was perhaps less than Derby raised a lot of red flags inside the organisation. While Kirchner was telling the world he would be the next owner of Derby County, in reality he had never once put any money into a UK bank account to show proof of funds. Nor had he put together a complete business plan to show he could run the club for a year to two years.

Despite those shortcomings, Kirchner announced that it was due to other difficulties with the takeover that he was stepping away from the deal and expressed great sadness at doing so.

Kirchner went off to try and complete a deal for Preston, but the change of heart left a sour taste in the mouths of many Derby fans, also mixed in with sadness and anger that their club was being left in limbo.

With Kirchner seemingly moving on to other things, the search for a new owner continued and a familiar wheeler-dealer reared his head once again. Mike Ashley had recently sold Newcastle United for £305m and was seemingly stepping away from football ownership for a while, perhaps for good. But then the opportunity to buy Derby came up. Ashley had made it clear he was seriously interested in purchasing the club but he was also adamant that he was going to drive a hard bargain, such were the issues he would have to tackle should he take ownership. Ashley had built a reputation for being two things: a tough negotiator, and playing 'moneyball' on transfers. Newcastle fans were fed up of Ashley buying cheap and selling high – a watermark of nearly all his business dealings in and out of football, until his final couple of Newcastle transfer windows where he spent heavily on the likes of Miguel Almirón and Joelinton. But for Derby, somebody who was tight with the purse strings and looked to get value signings was just the thing they needed.

Ashley's main concern was Pride Park Stadium. Morris was holding out to try and make some sort of return on his £81m purchase of it via one of his other companies and his valuation of it fluctuated depending on which reports you read. Anything from £20m to £40m was being quoted and it was a fee Ashley was not willing to pay considering the sizeable debts the club had racked up as well as the investment into the squad which would be required. Ashley was willing to bid £50m all told for the club and its assets, but other parties were holding out for a package closer to £60m.

In February 2022, Ashley's publicist and public relations advisor Keith Bishop said, 'He wants the Derby fans to know that he is interested in buying the club and that's why we've broken ranks today really. Mike's got a love of football and obviously his business is sport as well. So sport is connected to football. So he sees the good points of having football connected to his business and he still loves it.'

In the end, Ashley's interest did not exceed initial conversations about buying the club. No formal bid was ever made, nor was he ever selected as the preferred bidder, and while his name was constantly on the outskirts of the conversation it was understood that neither party would move from their valuation of the club – as evidenced when David Clowes eventually did step in with a £60m bid.

Kirchner, however, did have a second bite at the cherry – albeit with a caveat. He had privately told sections of people he was schmoozing that he would only re-enter negotiations on the basis of Carl Jenkinson being ostracised from the process. The relationship between the pair had broken down to such a degree that the American wished to no longer work alongside one of Quantuma's joint administrators.

With both Kirchner and Quantuma seemingly tip-toeing around each other, Kirchner made another bid for the club in April 2022 which was confirmed by a statement from the administrators, 'Following a rigorous and well-documented marketing process, the joint administrators of Derby County Football Club have accepted an offer from Chris Kirchner to acquire Derby County Football Club out of administration.'

The preferred bidder status gave Kirchner exclusivity in accessing all of the club's confidential accounts, and gave him preferential status to complete a takeover. Kirchner would attempt to broker a deal for the stadium personally with Mel Morris, but talks were difficult as Morris clung to his valuation of Pride Park and his firm belief that the stadium could be used for so much more than football matches.

As the old saying goes – once bitten, twice shy. Derby fans were still behind Kirchner, their feelings driven by pure worry for their club, but they had new concerns given his withdrawal from the process some four months earlier and his apparent courting of another club. Many believed he was not as sincere as he portrayed and was simply looking to add any club to his portfolio; Derby just happened to be the most attractive one.

What strengthened his case this time was the public support of manager Wayne Rooney, who said, 'He has got some really good ideas and as long as everything is right for the club I can see it being a real positive.

'It is important that we look and assess everything in the club and try and improve. Whether that is the stadium, training ground, players coming in, players signing new contracts. We have to have everything in place because that's what we need. He is a very good businessman and I am sure he wouldn't be putting his name to a public statement if he didn't mean what he is trying to do at the club.'

Kirchner and Rooney got on well. The pair of course had a mutual friend in Paul Stretford – Rooney's agent. Such was the nature of Stretford and Kirchner's relationship, Triple S Sports and Entertainment Group, which is co-owned by Stretford, were said to have covered wages in May 2022 to aid Kirchner's bid to become Derby owner.

Kirchner even took to Twitter to tell fans that he and Rooney would exchange WhatsApp messages almost daily and discuss all manner of things and even called Rooney 'the best young manager in the game', stating that his presence in the Pride Park dugout was one of the key reasons he decided to re-enter the race to buy the club. The public flattering of one another drew many to believe that a happy marriage would soon come once a takeover was completed. Kirchner was acting as Derby County's owner. He had all the garb including a club jacket and hat, he would attend games and would interact with the fans on Twitter. Kirchner was even invited to Moor Farm to be introduced to the squad.

Things got so far down the line that Kirchner and Quantuma exchanged contracts for the sale of the club in mid-May 2022 with Quantuma believing the takeover would be completed by the end of the month. That deadline was the third the administrators had set, with Kirchner missing the previous two for various reasons that included bank holidays in the US and the UK not allowing for the transfer of money between bank accounts.

The process dragged on until Quantuma informed Kirchner that he had been given until 5pm by the EFL on 10 June to produce proof of funds that he could purchase and run Derby County. The *Daily Mail* reported the takeover was on the verge of collapse as Kirchner could not demonstrate the money to close the deal.

However, having not met the deadline, a week later Kirchner withdrew his bid – stunning the EFL and Quantuma, who were both confident that the deal would be completed. Kirchner never did manage to successfully transfer the funds to the UK despite his repeated promises that he could do so.

The decision rocked the EFL to such a degree that they told Quantuma they now wished to be informed of all discussions with any other interested parties to ensure another such debacle did not occur – and with Derby's future teetering, they could not afford another such instance.

22

The March to Pride Park

AS THE Rams' plight continued, and with Quantuma continuously searching for, and failing to find, a buyer, and with the EFL demanding proof of funds that the club could be sustained for the rest of the season, by late January 2022 supporters were facing the very real prospect of their club folding. The sense of anger, hurt, nervousness and uncertainty was palpable.

Fans had had enough; they had become sick of what they felt was a lack of transparency by the club. When Stephen Pearce was going on the radio to declare that the BZI takeover was almost done yet those close to the deal believed it was always dead in the water – what were they meant to believe? When Quantuma were communicating messages when it suited them, such as deadline dates and if hard deadlines were ever set – they claimed they were, others claimed they were more frameworks and not hard deadlines – then supporters were, naturally, going to be either scared, angry, worried, or everything in between. It was time for action. Fans felt they had no choice but to mobilise to get their message across loud and clear – they were not to be taken lightly and would not go down without a fight.

Ahead of the Rams' home fixture with Birmingham on 30 January 2022, thousands of fans organised a march from the city centre to Pride Park as part of the 'Save Derby County' campaign. The march was to start at 11.30am and end outside the home ground ahead of the 1.30pm kick-off. It was estimated around 1,000 people would turn up, but on the day around 10,000 supporters were shown marching in solidarity, with flags, banners, songs and painted torsos – the cold winter air bothering them little as they marched proud as punch towards Pride Park and getting national and local media attention, using their own social media platforms to spread awareness of the march. For many, they truly believed it would be the final time they got to see their club play a game of football, and they wanted to go out with the biggest statement possible – you cannot kill the spirit of Derby County.

The match itself was riddled with tension, worry and nerves – but also defiance, spirit, togetherness and a feeling that everybody connected with the club who was powerless in the situation was one united force. Pride Park was sold out – with thousands more packing the streets and pubs to watch the game and give their support.

The day threatened to end in disappointment when Derby went 2-0 down before the hour mark. Some players attested to the occasion overwhelming them in the early stages, and the emotion from the fans adding extra pressure to want to get a result for them. Yet even when facing a two-goal deficit, the mood refused to be soured as fans showed their biggest sign of support for a club on its knees.

But much like the supporters had done, and the players had continued to do throughout the season – they found

242

something. Derby dug deep and snatched a 2-2 draw courtesy of two late goals from Luke Plange and Krystian Bielik. Bielik's effort – a 93rd-minute overhead kick after which it was feared he had dislocated his shoulder in attempting – sent everybody wild: fans, and players on the pitch, who took a moment to realise Bielik was hurt. Rooney was also in euphoria on the sidelines and marvelling at his side's never-say-die attitude. The Derby faithful left Pride Park going bonkers but the day as a whole was an emotional drain and a fight for hope. The stories of the fans piece together one of the most momentous days in the club's history, so the remainder of this chapter is told through their eyes.

* * *

Aaron Mansfield: 'It was, obviously, a really emotional time for us all. My grandad has taken me to games since I was five and I still go with him now at 31. I've never had contact with my dad and I think that somehow made all those Saturday afternoons even more special, having that time together with my grandad, doing that kind of stuff.

'On the day of the march, me and my grandad parked up at the train station as usual and waited for the march to come over the flyover so we could join it. Thinking about the sight of the march coming over the top of the hill still gives me instant goosebumps. We joined the march when it reached us, and it was even more jaw-dropping to look back five minutes later to see that the flow of people hadn't stopped.

'On a basic level, there was something so instantly cathartic in knowing that all these people around you were experiencing the exact same maelstrom of feelings that you were. It sounds cheesy, but it really felt like the moment at which the cavalry came and we sort of said, "If you want to take this away from us, you're going to have to come through us all.'"

* * *

Joe Farmer: 'Coming into Derby you could feel something was different from any ordinary matchday warm-up. Walking towards where the march was planned to start, you could feel the atmosphere building. It felt like everyone was building up to something important, yet at the same time you could feel the anxiety. When more people arrived it built momentum and turned the mood into a collective, spirited and uplifting one on the whole.

'I genuinely couldn't believe it. My dad and I were towards the front of the march, we saw what felt like thousands of fans snake round the junction and up towards the bridge where we were standing. We thought that the number and size of the crowd couldn't continue to grow, but we were so wrong, it was very emotional. I've never been so proud of this club and the fans. Seeing what it meant to so many also had such a profound impact on myself. I genuinely had the feeling like it could be one of the last times supporting my club and being surrounded by my extended Rams family.'

* * *

Chris Clewlow: 'I was gearing up for what possibly could have been one of the biggest walks of my life: making a statement to save our football club. On the morning of the march I tested positive for Covid. I was gutted. I watched the march from home keeping up to date on social media and TV. I have never been more proud to be a fan of Derby County Football Club. The amount of people, the noise, the passion. I really do feel the point was made, we cannot let this football club die. We got more national media attention and a lot of interest from other fans. Fair play to the guys that organised it.'

* * *

Yardie Ram on Twitter: 'That day was magic. The togetherness in the city, from the town centre to the stadium, catching up with old friends, meeting new ones and that whole crowd there in that moment because we all share the same passion for this club.

'Then for the game to go how it went, 2-0 down looking like it was going to dampen the day's mood, to see the togetherness that we had as fans transpire on to the pitch through each and every person involved in the club, was an indescribable feeling. The fightback, the pushback, it was a message to the football world that we simply will not give up, we won't roll over, we just won't die as a club.

'People's faces and moods were just amazing to see and feel after that, it gave us that good times feeling, it was just the beginning of our club's fight back, what a day, what a moment.'

* * *

Dan Wilson: 'I've been a Derby fan for 34 years. My grandad took me to the Baseball Ground, my dad took me to Pride Park, and I've been going with friends since I was

14 or so. The whole administration affected me massively. I have a son, and at the time he was only four and had never been to a live match. The thought of the club dying without him getting to experience a game killed me, and I marched for him. Derby is in your blood, it's a family tradition and going to games is much more than just 90 minutes of football.

'The pride and togetherness I felt on that march is something I will never forget, and the limbs after the Bielik equaliser is something I'll remember until the day I die.'

* * *

Jacob Watson: 'It was honestly the moment I realised just how big a football club I support. I've been going to games since I was six. I've seen big attendances and multiple play-off heartbreaks. But that day, being in that sea of people walking was when I realised just how much Derby County means to the fans and everyone in the city, it was just mental. Walking under the underpass near the bus station and hearing the echoes of the chanting fans was an unforgettable experience. The day came with a sense of absolute dread at the same time though. But nothing can take away from the pride I had for our fanbase and then the game afterwards unfolding the way it did, whilst we didn't win, it was just an immense and emotional day.'

* * *

Nick Watson: 'The first thing that sticks in my mind from that day was the fusion of contemporary and history. You had flags with "Mel Morris Club Killer" next to images of Brian Clough, Arthur Cox and Jim Smith. It felt like we were not only saying "Please someone save our club" but "Who do you think you are? Using our club with its community and history as a toy, putting something so sacred at risk of extinction."

'The second thing is I was with my brother and a couple of his mates, and throughout we were trying to work out how many people were actually there. We were right in the middle so it was hard to see the full scale, until we went over the bridge on Pride Park Way and could see in front and behind us thousands of people. Genuinely breathtaking.'

* * *

Andy Hardy: 'My parents are in their 80s but were determined to be part of the march. They wanted to represent their generation and be with their family, supporting a club that has been part of all our lives for so long. They joined us about 100 yards from Pride Park and walked proudly to the stadium with family and friends from all over the country. Derby is more than just football, it's about families and friends getting together and sharing a common love.'

* * *

James Aspinall: 'I went on the March with my mum, dad and little sister. It was my little sister's first league game, she'd been to friendlies before but this was her first league game. Had her on my shoulders the whole way, singing her heart out. Said she hopes it isn't her last game.'

* * *

Marie Strawther: 'We marched as a group of ten season ticket holders and three generations of family, with the eldest 69 years old and the youngest eight years old. The march represented everything that our football club stands for: family, togetherness and the community of our city. I've never felt prouder to be a Ram or more as one with the city and club. The sight of the march on the bridge took your breath away. I waited to join the march as it came over the bridge, and felt both proud and incredibly tearful.'

* * *

Joe Farmer: 'I genuinely had the feeling like it could be one of the last times supporting my club and being surrounded by my extended Rams family.'

* * *

Richard Leighton-Cox: 'I went into the day wondering whether that might be the last time I ever saw Derby play. With all the off-field worries and the deadlines shifting all the time, limited progress and little communication made that day feel like a real statement that the fans were going to remain united and would fight for the club. The whole thing went beyond football and the club itself and represented what Derby County as a community means to so many people across the country. It was a real sense of togetherness and reiterated that the club could not be left to die. To put on a real show that the fans were the driving force was a really proud moment, and it's something that I'll personally always be glad to have been a part of.'

* * *

Jacob Bagguley: 'The march was unreal. Nearly 10,000 of our fans came together to stop our club from dying. The noise we created and the atmosphere while walking to Pride Park was immense. It was emotional as it was potentially our last game as a club and it was making me fall out of love with football. The whole fan base banded together to try and stop our club from dying and to let everybody know how much this club means to so many people.'

* * *

Gavin Atkins: 'I was absolutely compelled to attend even though I didn't expect that many to be there. When I turned up it was obvious that this was going to be a special day. Being part of that march is something I'm very proud of as it was us fans standing up in defiance to Morris and the EFL and showing them what this club means to us. Watching the drone footage back brought a tear to my eye. I felt like I was attending on behalf of my children as well as myself. We were so close to that being taken away from the future generations of fans.

'I like to think that day made a difference and kept our situation in focus, or more to the point brought it into focus on the likes of Sky. It felt like we had been screaming in space for months and all we got back was radio silence. Looking at where we are now and where we were at that point, it makes that day even more important.'

* * *

George Whittaker: 'I'd never seen such togetherness as a football club. It started off as something quite small on

Twitter, and I wasn't sure it would get that much traction. There was mention of closing the A52 for the event a few days before, which made me think it may be bigger than I first thought. But nothing prepared me for how big it actually was. It was insane; when standing on the A52 overpass all you could see for half a mile in front and a mile behind was Derby fans.

'Although it was a time of huge frustration, anger and worry for fans, the march itself was very upbeat. Most fans were singing, lots had banners, flares, there was a band towards the front. I think it was a good way of fans showing their frustration towards the situation, but also backing the boys on the pitch at the same time.

'Although it was just me and my mate who went, we saw people we knew along the way and chatted with a few others, so it wasn't like it was just us. It was a shame we couldn't get a win, but the scenes for the equaliser were incredible. Overall it was a great day and a good statement for the football club.'

* * *

Mark Stewart: 'I was shocked at how many people were already gathered at the Market Place – we thought we were early. It was very good-natured – chatting to people you'd never seen before, in between the singing.

'When the march actually started moving it was actually quite surreal! When we passed the Council House, the mayor shook mine and Alex's hand – Ruby thought it was a random bloke in fancy dress. Later on, the echoing sound of the singing as we passed under the Cock Pitt car park on Morledge gave me shivers. It was other-worldly.

'The next incredible moment was going up the flyover, past the back of Castle Park Nursing Home. A 91-year-old lady called Betty was standing in the window with a couple of staff absolutely loving it. She was clapping and waving to everyone, and that's when the tears came for me. I hadn't long since lost my mum, who ended her time in a similar place. I feel blessed to have shared the experience with my daughters. I know just how much following Derby means to Alex, and the thought of it possibly being taken away was horrific.'

* * *

Jack Carter: 'I was so tense throughout the whole game as it felt like the perfect statement to say, "We're still here and it'll take a lot more than you think to take Derby County away from us", but the game, as was the same with our club, was slipping away from us. I was sat with my old man as I had done for the last 25 years when that cross came in and Bielik thundered home that bicycle kick. It felt like I was thrown back into being five years old celebrating with my dad, who I'm sure in turn felt like he was back five years old with his dad at the Baseball Ground. It truly reminded me of why the club wasn't just a Saturday at 3pm job, but generations of memories with friends and family.'

* * *

Gareth Watson: 'Living away from Derby was especially hard during the administration and takeover period. I genuinely felt helpless. However, where some fans would've sought some comfort from family members or friends I didn't have that living so far away, and you can only get so much from social media.

'So when the Birmingham match was touted as potentially our last-ever match I knew I needed to be there. Regardless of what we had planned as a family that weekend, I knew that simply doing the march was needed even if I didn't get a ticket to the match. Luckily I secured tickets and travelled down with a good friend. Funnily enough, it was the first time we met in real life, having struck up a friendship in the months prior.

'Walking towards the assembly rooms where the march was starting was something else. You could hear the crowd from a mile away.

'The only thing that came close to that noise was at Wembley prior to play-off final games.

'We marched about 25 rows behind the front so didn't really have an idea of the scale of it. The singing in the underpass near the Eagle Centre was incredible but the moment where the scale of it all hit me was when we stopped on the railway bridge and looked back at the crowd. Goosebumps. I'll never forget that moment and it was a privilege to be a part of it. These were all my people! It brought it home right then that we couldn't lose this magnificent club.'

* * *

Matt Freeman: 'The day itself felt rather surreal as me, my brother and my dad felt it could be the last time we ever saw the club play. It was one of sadness, but also brought up some fantastic memories of years gone by.

'We weren't quite sure what to expect from the march and the day itself, but to see and hear the city and the club more united in that moment was something truly special.

From that moment on, the unity between the club and the fans has been non-stop.'

* * *

Heather Kirk: 'After not being able to go and watch our beloved team because of Covid, the sudden thought that we might lose the club completely was heartbreaking. The march was unifying, and showed the depth of feeling, what the club means, and the one love for our club that we share. I marched because we needed to make it known that we were not going to let this happen quietly.

'I was proud of my home city that day, proud to be from there, and proud to be part of a fanbase that can come together in a crisis, that can raise funds to pay off debts to St John Ambulance – a debt that should never have been allowed to happen.'

* * *

Davey Walker: 'I'd always wanted to take my daughter to a Derby match and have experiences I didn't get with my own dad. I ensured I took her that day because I was legitimately concerned I may not get another chance.

'We started in town just to view the march and my daughter was so excited by all the atmosphere. We started making our way to the stadium but ended up in the march and just stayed in it. You could feel the emotion within the crowd. My daughter turned to me and said, "I love this, I've never seen so many people before at a football match."

'When that equaliser from Bielik went in it was unbelievable. I saw fans crying. Was this the last Rams goal we would ever see? We celebrated like it was.'

23

Relegation

DERBY HAD battled valiantly in the face of constant adversity off the field, but also on the field as the shallowness of the squad finally started to catch up with them as 2021/22 progressed. Still there was hope. A 2-0 victory over Sheffield United, a 3-1 triumph over Hull City, and the seeming ability to turn 2-0 deficits into 2-2 draws – such as against Reading and Birmingham City – meant the Rams gave themselves a realistic fighting chance entering the final stretch of the season. But picking up the occasional win was no longer enough – Derby needed to put together a run and just when they got a positive result it would be followed up by a string of defeats. The surprise win over Sheffield United in January was followed up by a string of three defeats in which Derby conceded two goals in each of them. The 1-0 victory over Peterborough United in February was followed up with three defeats. Then the Rams would record a 2-0 win over Barnsley at the start of March – only to go on another winless run of three.

Regardless of the defeats and increasing slide into what felt like inevitability, Wayne Rooney was quick to remind everybody – rightly so – that the points total was not an accurate reflection on what his team had produced and mentally everybody needed to add an extra 21 points on to their total; as well as the 12 points automatically deducted for going into administration, a further nine were taken off in November after the club admitted breaching EFL accounting rules. Practically and in reality, those mental add-ons did not equate to being safely in mid-table. But psychologically it helped the players focus and remember how good they were, and aided them when trying to put a run together to pull off one of the greatest escapes in English football history.

'I think it helped in a way. Sometimes when you're at the bottom and miles off the pace you can look at it and believe the group isn't good enough to compete,' Curtis Davies said. 'But that wasn't the case with us. We knew we could compete. We knew we had a team that could pick up points – it was just a matter of whether we could put that run together in time and get 12 points out of 15. We knew that would be a tall order but we'd done it just a couple months before over Christmas and new year.

'I think the season just physically took its toll on the boys. It was a thin squad, a lot of young lads with little experience or older boys where it was maybe a stretch to play 90 minutes three times a week and be as effective as they'd been in the first part of the season. So we'd get a win, but it would take so much out of us, then we'd lost three on the bounce. And in the predicament we were in, we couldn't really afford to do that.'

The victory against Barnsley was a vital one – it signified tremendous hope with ten games left to play. Even after the two points deductions and being plunged to the bottom of the Championship, Derby had somehow picked themselves up and got within eight points of survival after beating the Tykes. It wasn't that the task was easily achievable. Or even that it was a touch challenging – the job in front of them was their biggest mountain to scale. One that, with the squad depth issues, some regarded as almost – but not completely – impossible. That they had given themselves a fighting chance was all they could have asked for at that stage of the season.

Even as their own results faltered and time was cut from ten games to six, there was still the faint snick of hope that they could pull off a miraculous escape as Reading had only extended the points deficit from eight to nine due to their own struggles, which also included a six-point deduction. But the stakes were increasingly becoming do or die after a 2-1 defeat at Swansea City – and the Rams' next opponents were not in the mood to be handing out lifelines. Fulham were chasing their return to the Premier League in style by going up as champions, and a Good Friday win at Pride Park would have cemented their status. Rooney, however, had always stressed the importance of playing against the big teams and his sides often equipped themselves well against more expansive opponents, such was their own desire to play stylish football.

Fulham were frustrated for the opening exchanges as Derby sat deep and looked to counter – but they broke through in the 20th minute to leave the Rams on the brink, and their own promotion hopes on a different sort of brink. However, Rooney didn't panic. He stressed at half-time that his players should continue playing with courage, insisting that Fulham would present his team with opportunities, that they could be got at down the sides and that Derby had the quality to hurt them. He also reminded them of the mountains they had already overcome to give themselves a flicker of hope of survival.

In the end, two goals – both coming down the flanks – turned the game on its head resulting in a highly unlikely victory for Derby, with young Luke Plange being the man of the moment with first the equaliser, and then pressure on Tosin Adarabioyo who turned it into his own net, although Plange would have tapped in had the Fulham defender not obliged first.

'Character – that's it,' Rooney said afterwards. 'We've had it all season. It was difficult today with all the teams around us winning or drawing. This is a young group of players and it's a test for their character. I felt we could win the game at half-time. We pressed higher and made it more difficult for them to play out. We deserved the three points. We were excellent. There's a small chance. We will fight right until the end.'

How brutal it was, then, that the end came in the very next game in the most heartbreaking fashion at the Kiyan Prince Foundation Stadium against Queens Park Rangers. Rooney's side went there knowing a defeat and any positive result for Reading would condemn them to English football's third tier for the first time since 1986. Derby attacked QPR with gusto as if their very lives were on the line and had an added slice of fortune with Swansea going 3-1 up against Reading at half-time. As Derby huffed and puffed to find a goal which would keep their faint Championship survival hopes alive for at least one more week, Reading were slipping into further trouble when going 4-1 down before the hour mark – before an incredible, gut-wrenching, heartbreaking scene played out. Former Derby winger Tom Ince gave the Royals some life, reducing the scoreline against Swansea to 4-2. No danger so far; there was still a mountain to climb for them and Derby were still being held and probing for the game's first goal. With 20 minutes to play, Reading scored again to reduce the deficit to 4-3. All season long Swansea had shown a propensity to ship goals – some of them as soft as marshmallows, and it was now creeping in to not only quieten their own fans, but make Derby supporters extremely nervous as both games reached their climax. Then came the double blow which served as a large exclamation point on the season. QPR scored. The hosts worked the ball down the right and dragged Curtis Davies and Eiran Cashin across leaving a gap behind them for Luke Amos to stroll into without a Derby shirt within five yards of him and slot the ball past Ryan Allsop with just two minutes remaining. Derby could escape for one more week if Swansea could hold on to their lead at Reading. But they couldn't. With virtually the last kick Reading levelled the score at 4-4 to compound the breaking hearts in black and white.

After the game Rooney was swelled with pride, and directed his anger and frustrations at one man – Mel Morris. With relegation came clarity, and also a strange sense of pride.

'I feel proud,' Rooney said with a courageous smile on his face. 'It's a strange feeling. Everything we've been through as a group: the lads on the pitch, the staff, the fans. All the development as a group – there are so many positives. We've been relegated, but I've never seen a team get relegated and that's the reaction of the fans. It was incredible the support the fans have given the lads all season. So I'm disappointed, upset, but I'm also proud.

'In some ways we can draw a line under everything that's happened. We can really start the rebirth of this club and move this club forward. We need this takeover to happen quickly. We know what division we'll be in next season and the quicker we can develop the squad and bring players into the squad we can get the club back up. If the takeover happens – and that has to happen – I want to rebuild the club.

'I feel for the players more [than myself]. We've picked up 52 points and we'd be safe in normal circumstances. We've paid the price of what the previous owner has left behind. It's no one's fault – not mine, not the staff, it's the previous owner. And it's a sad day for him as well because I know Mel is a Derby fan, and I'm sure he'll be very disappointed.'

There were four more matches to play before the season concluded, after which the players had a debrief and departed for their holidays with the vast majority knowing they would not be back for 2022/23. Ravel Morrison was open to the idea of remaining after having his most successful season and working with Rooney, whom he respected a lot. But his staying largely depended on whether his manager also stuck around. Allsop was out of contract and had been receiving interest from Championship clubs, while backup shot-stopper Kelle Roos's time at the club had seemed to be up months earlier and he would also be moving on once his contract expired. Tom Lawrence's contract expired and he left for pastures new with Rangers who had just qualified for the group stages of the Champions League following their Scottish Premiership title victory – a move nobody at Derby resented after the Wales international had stitched together perhaps his most complete performances under Rooney's watch. And Krystian Bielik was making his feelings clear that he wanted to move on to realise his dream of playing for Poland at the 2022 Qatar World Cup the following winter.

Colin Kazim-Richards was also quietly not offered a fresh contract and was let go. Rooney had been trying to replace him since the end of 2020/21, but financial handcuffs meant he had to rely on the former Celtic frontman for at least one more season. However, Kazim-Richards suffered an Achilles injury at the start of the campaign, which sidelined him for three months, and after that he never really got going again save for a three-game spell around Christmas. That he was constantly coming off the bench – like a flashback to the final Phillip Cocu days, with equally futile results in how he was used – also didn't help keep the striker fit or happy. An ankle injury in March against Blackburn Rovers put paid to his season but in truth he, Rooney and Rosenior were not seeing eye to eye with regards to how much playing time he should get, what he could offer the team and if he was to stay on for life in League One.

'They did Colin a bit dirty on the way out,' a former coach said. 'He'd given them everything, pushed through the pain barrier and scored some vital goals for them.

However, I would say at times he could be difficult to work with. That larger-than-life personality was needed in the dressing room, but it also came with some challenges – that challenge being sometimes he wasn't very receptive to another decision or opinion. Colin is a top bloke – but ego can sometimes cloud his judgement.'

Later in the summer, Nathan Byrne, who won the club's players' player of the year award, looked to be staying put before pre-season when the *Derby Telegraph* reported the defender was looking to walk away from his contract in a similar fashion to Lee Buchanan. Byrne wished to exercise his right under Transfer of Undertakings to leave following the club's takeover. Derby had initially triggered Byrne's 12-month extension – a move that had been backed by the EFL. However, because the club had been moved to a new company following Clowes Developments' purchase, it is governed by legislation known as the Transfer of Undertakings (TUPE).

In simple terms, while employees are automatically switched to the new company, they have the right under TUPE to be told about the transfer and can object to the move meaning they effectively resign. It is the same route that Buchanan took to leave for Werder Bremen. Derby did eventually receive an undisclosed amount of compensation for Buchanan from the Bundesliga club, but it was safe to say that both departures left a sour taste in the mouths of not only the fans, but several squad members who felt the pair had not gone in the best possible manner, and felt let down after all the group had gone through together.

With the mass exodus of players, a takeover still not in sight and Rooney getting increasingly twitchy about the season ahead, Derby may have had the answers as to which division they'd be playing in for 2022/23 but they were no closer to answering many of the more pressing questions, until the 11th hour.

24

Enter Clowes

IT SEEMED that Mel Morris had exercised all his potential options. Derby were teetering on the edge and were within ten days of going out of existence while Morris was unable to find a willing buyer at any price at all. The EFL were also considering every possible alternative, including, among other scenarios, Derby going out of the EFL and having to essentially start their journey all over again from the ground up, or beginning their League One season with a points deduction.

Conversations continued with Mike Ashley, whom both Quantuma and the EFL believed to have legitimate interest, but the former Newcastle United owner was not budging from the concerns he had about ownership of the stadium, the amount of debt to be paid back to HMRC and the overall investment needed in the squad. However, he seemed to be Derby's best hope due to how he ran Newcastle United for 14 years. While it was not the most ambitious project and his penny-pinching approach by turning everything about Newcastle United corporate and making it a pure money-making machine had installed a deep resentment from every Newcastle fan, he at least displayed he could keep a sustainable business model – which is what the EFL found most attractive. But movement from his side was not forthcoming. That was when David Clowes stepped in.

Clowes, a Derby fan through and through and a North Stand season ticket holder at Pride Park, did not want to see his hometown club go under but also was well aware of the situation he would inherit. He was under no illusion that a squad would have to be put together quickly and a business plan with the EFL would have to be agreed as to the financial parameters the club would be placed under for the following two years – contracts of a maximum of two years could be offered to players, along with a wage cap to ensure the club could be run sustainably. The parameters were seen as sensible for the foreseeable future by both the club and the EFL, and both parties were open to discussing them again should Derby go up at the first time of asking.

Clowes owning Derby felt like history coming back around some two decades later. The Clowes family very nearly took over the club in 2002 when Clowes's father was approached with the offer of buying Derby but it never transpired. Indeed, his 2023 takeover was not the first time that David had been approached about buying the club. He had previously turned down opportunities to mount a bid, but had never fully shut the door on the idea, and with Derby in dire straits he felt it the right time to step in. Clowes was not after being labelled a saviour – he was simply doing what he thought any fan with his resources would do and help bring the club out of a dark period. But that was not so straightforward.

Clowes opened discussions with Chris Kirchner's people – Garry Cook and Paul Stretford – to ask if they were serious about stepping away so the local property businessman could step in and take the reins.

Morris and Clowes then got properly introduced in early June. The two knew of each other prior to sitting down to discuss the sale of the club, but never really struck up any kind of relationship until then. Morris liked Clowes's business acumen, that he was a property expert and thus knew the true value of Pride Park Stadium and how to maintain it and develop it. By 17 June the stadium was sold to Clowes for £22m, coming at a time when Kirchner's bid finally collapsed. Clowes and Morris agreed that if Derby had a home to play in then it would be halfway to saving the club. Despite reports that the sale of the stadium was holding up previous takeovers and putting off other potential suitors – such as Mike Ashley – the sale proved to be the smoothest part of the transition.

After that, it was time to sort out the debts and the rest of the assets the club had. After working out a deal with HMRC over the tax debt, as well as MSD Holdings, the rest of the club was eventually sold for £38m – which many believed to be excessive and even Clowes himself accepted that he overpaid, but did not see another option outside of letting one of the founding members of the Football League go out of business.

Clowes presented his business plan to the EFL and, in the process, made chief executive Stephen Pearce an integral part of the process in a show of faith to Pearce – who had often been at the mercy of a bullish and often reckless Morris when it came to business dealings. The relationship between Derby and the EFL had become greatly fractured during Morris's tenure, often engaging in wars of words and acts of brinkmanship. Clowes wanted to repair the relationship and become more transparent with the organisation – part of that being scheduling regular check-ins with EFL chief executive Trevor Birch.

The deal was delayed by a full week as Clowes attempted to undo some of the promises made in bad faith by Kirchner – including promising trustees of the training ground a percentage of the land. After those had been smoothed over, Clowes set to work. But he had to navigate a managerial change pretty early into his tenure.

Rooney had hitched his wagon to Kirchner. The two had a mutual friend in Paul Stretford and Rooney was banking on the American taking over, with Stretford at the helm and recruiting players he wanted. Many saw it as a chance for the former Manchester United striker to consolidate his power within the club.

However, when the deal fell through and Clowes was on the brink of officially taking over, Rooney resigned. In a statement released on 24 June 2022, he said, 'Over the course of the summer I have been closely following developments regarding the ownership of Derby County. Today I met with the administrators to inform them of my decision that it was time for me to leave the club. In fairness to them, they tried tremendously hard to change my decision but my mind was made up.

'Personally, I feel the club now needs to be led by someone with fresh energy and not affected by the events that have happened over the last 18 months.'

Although his tenure ended with relegation to his name, Rooney could rightly point to the overall points total he achieved as manager in his final season as being enough to plonk Derby squarely in mid-table. That, for him, was fulfilling enough for him to seek pastures new. He was happy with how things ended at Derby, but was also not actively seeking a break in his managerial career as evidenced by him becoming manager of DC United just 18 days later.

On 1 July 2022, David Clowes completed his takeover of Derby County Football Club. The speed at which the takeover was achieved, the EFL believed, was evidence that had any of the BZI, Alonso and the two Kirchner bids been seriously credible, a deal could have been wrapped up in a matter of weeks.

Quantuma released a joint statement through the club which in part read:

'Quantuma joint administrators, Andrew Hosking, Carl Jackson and Andrew Andronikou are delighted to confirm the completion of the sale of the business and assets of Derby County Football Club ('The Club') to Derbyshire based property group, Clowes Developments (UK) Ltd ('Clowes') for an undisclosed amount.

'The transaction sees the Club exit from administration and be brought under the same ownership structure as its stadium, Pride Park.

'Joint administrator, Carl Jackson said, "We are very pleased to have achieved today's sale, in a deal which secures the long-term future of The Club, and one which represents the very best outcome for creditors. I would like to express my sincere thanks to The Club's staff players and the fans for their loyalty, and patience, as they supported the Club through the administration."

'Joint administrator, Andrew Hosking added, "The level of complexity involved in bringing this matter to a conclusion has been unparalleled and we are grateful to all stakeholders and their advisers, for their hard work which has enabled us to overcome a magnitude of challenges, and allow the rescue of this historic Club. This deal represents a real milestone in the long and illustrious history of Derby County, and one which marks the end of the uncertainty experienced by supporters and the wider community whilst the club has been in administration and also importantly is one which complies with the EFL Insolvency Policy and provides the best return for creditors. Today signifies a new beginning for the Club, and it enables the Club to move forward into the new season with a clean slate, under local ownership under the stewardship of Clowes."'

Now not only did the club need a whole host of new players – they had just five under contract as they returned for pre-season in July 2022 – but they also required a new manager.

Liam Rosenior was installed on an interim basis and set about recruiting a squad. Rosenior had risen through the ranks from coach to assistant manager at the club and Clowes felt the time was right to reward him for his loyalty by giving him the top job, even if it was on a temporary deal. All involved felt it was a win-win. Derby were coming out of a fragile period and needed a stabiliser of sorts, but one without a serious financial commitment like Morris had given Phillip Cocu. Rosenior had intimate knowledge of the club and had also served his apprenticeship across the previous three seasons.

Rosenior opened his contact book and used his relationships to recruit as well as retain players. Curtis Davies was one of the first major acquisitions – or re-signings. Davies had been out of contract during the summer but gave Derby first refusal when it came to him negotiating his next deal. The defender was in no rush to find a new club and wanted to see how the Rams' situation played out. If Rosenior were to stay then it would swing the pendulum in favour of Davies staying at Pride Park, such was their closeness. The two were engaged in contract talks throughout the summer, with Davies rejecting the first offer of a flat one-year deal which didn't replicate his own valuation of himself within the team. The contract was not simply about money; Davies wanted assurances that he would be around the club for longer than one more year. At 37 he had more games behind him than in front of him and wanted more stability. Ambassadorial roles were discussed as were potential routes into coaching and while both sides' representatives worked away in the background both Davies and Rosenior were quietly confident the deal would be over the line within a week. On 8 July Davies put pen to paper.

With the captain tied back down for another season and at least some continuity in a squad that was about to experience mass changes, Rosenior got to work once more. In total, 11 free agent signings came in with a further four loans. The likes of former Sheffield United striker David McGoldrick, ex-Aston Villa midfielder Conor Hourihane, and Brighton & Hove Albion loanee defender Haydon

Roberts all said that Rosenior was a big pull for them in moving to Pride Park. Though Rosenior lacked true top-level managerial experience, he still possessed the people skills and thick contacts book to make moves in the market.

The squad did not have much of a pre-season together and had to build chemistry and cohesion on the fly, which manifested early in the results. Derby opened up their 2022/23 season with a 1-0 victory over Oxford United at a sold-out Pride Park. It was an encouraging performance with obvious room for growth. Growing pains came to the fore quickly, however – and with the club trying to come out of a fragile position Rosenior's grasp on his job became less iron-clad. Not that he was in any immediate danger of getting the sack, but internally questions were starting to be asked about how much risk was attached to their rookie manager.

The biggest early problems were goals and away form – the two going hand in hand. Derby failed to score a single goal in their first four League One away matches and did not enjoy an away win in the competition until 1 October – when Rosenior was no longer in charge. The former Hull City defender was relieved of his duties on 21 September, during the international break and just six days after Derby had registered a 2-1 home win over Wycombe Wanderers, after seven victories from 12 matches in all competitions.

The announcement shocked some of the players and even Rosenior himself, who had been quietly confident that his interim role would be made permanent. Some close to him even suggested that he had disclosed that a permanent contract was on the table and just needed his solicitor to go over the details. However, internal discussions led to Clowes and company wanting to mitigate any risk – and Rosenior's rookie status as a manager was a risk the club could reduce if the right opportunity came along.

After the announcement that Rosenior was no longer the interim manager, he originally stayed as a coach, but once Paul Warne was confirmed as manager Rosenior left Pride Park. Clowes and Rosenior had discussions and the pair maintained a strong relationship, with Clowes giving Rosenior a handsome payout and also a glowing recommendation for the Hull City job when he interviewed for it. Rosenior was in an unfortunate position. Some connected with Derby County felt that he was the last bastion of a previous era and it would be beneficial for the long-term health of the club if as much of that era as possible was moved along to truly allow the Rams to move on. Warne and Clowes clicked right away. The pair shared common interests and very similar outlooks on life – that is not to say Clowes and Rosenior did not, but Warne, three times a promotion winner from League One with Rotherham United, struck a certain chord with Clowes that compelled him to make the move and install him as manager.

25

Warne-ing to the Rest of the Division

DERBY'S PLAYERS were slightly shocked to learn of Liam Rosenior's dismissal on 27 September 2022. 'I thought he was getting the job to be honest,' Curtis Davies said. 'I was shocked and gutted for Liam and not just because of my relationship with him, but because I thought he'd done a good job in the games that he had – and he'd also done so much of the recruitment.

'I think we were a bit disappointed that Liam had pieced together this team to build something in his identity; we'd made all these signings to fit a certain manager's style – and then that manager is relieved of his duties. Obviously the club had been through so much negativity in the recent years and Rosey [Rosenior] was one of the ones that had stuck around and seen it through with the club. I understand he was an interim, but ultimately he still signed players to help his style of play. He spent the summer with the analysts and the staff to make sure we had a team. It was a tough pill to swallow when he went.'

That did not mean that Davies held any ill will against the incoming Paul Warne. Manager arrivals and departures are as routine in football as there only being one ball, and the decisions were taken from higher up. And when Warne and Davies met, the duo would quickly grow to like each other.

'Regardless of your personal relationships with any manager, ultimately this is a new guy [Warne] and a new start,' Davies said. 'So the boys who weren't playing were thinking now was the time to go and impress him, and the boys who were in the squad had to prove it all over again – so everybody was at it.

'What helped with the transition though from Liam to Paul was just how nice a guy Paul is. I'm a chatterbox and even Paul gave me a run for my money. You can't help but love the guy. He's a great guy, great energy about him, and a really good person. He's honest, great humility, thoughtful, he's very philosophical because he knows he's an emotional person and therefore tries to be philosophical in his thinking to help stay calm.

'I think what also factored into it was quite simply he's been successful at League One level. Before last season [2022/23] he'd been promoted from League One every time he was in it as a manager. He knows how to get out of the league.'

While Rosenior was a hands-on style of coach on the training ground, Warne would delegate to his staff – assistant head coach Richie Barker, first-team coach Matt Hamshaw and first-team goalkeeper coach Andy Warrington.

Warne's iteration of Derby County looked a lot different to the one Rosenior was building. Rosenior's model was about possession, patience and build-up through the middle. Warne predominantly wanted to play with a back three, use the flanks more and have a pair of strikers up front – one usually dropping in to create an extra midfielder. But of course with that stylistic change came teething problems. In the summer, the club had recruited to accommodate Rosenior's style of play, and now the manager and style had changed.

'The style was chalk and cheese at first,' Davies said. 'With Liam – he was the coach, the manager and everything on the training ground. And in terms of style, we wanted a lot of the ball and to play with a back four. Whereas at Rotherham, with all respect to them, they had a way of doing things – which had obviously served them very well, especially at League One level. But the personnel was different.

'I think the biggest difference in terms of training style is that Paul is a manager, not a coach, in the way he goes about things. He lets his coaches and assistants get on with things mainly. He'll join in when we're doing shape work. He likes to get involved with the strikers and doing crossing work – but he openly admits that he is not the coach, Richie Barker is the primary coach on the field.

'With the style – Warne has always played with the thinking of why use 15 passes to get it forward when we can get it forward in two? So he wants it up the pitch quicker and wants us to play from the final third. That had to be drilled into us, because when we played under Liam we were still trying to play out from the back and tempt the opposition to come out of position before we created an opportunity.

'Under Paul, we did still want the ball, but it was more important to get it in the right territory now.

That was an adjustment. I think at first we were being too literal with how we played. Warne would ask us to play down the channels – so for a while some of the lads would be getting the ball out of their feet and just smashing it down the channel even if nobody was there, or there was no pressure on the ball carrier. The first few games was all about getting used to the different way of doing things.'

Warne's tenure got off to a decent start with a 2-0 away victory over Cambridge United, which served as a trifecta of goodness – first win for Warne, first away win and first away goals scored, for that matter, that season. That it took until 1 October was not ideal; poor away form had been one of the main concerns the hierarchy had with Rosenior. At the end of Rosenior's tenure, Derby were sniffing around the play-off places but it was felt that with a manager with more experience in the division – and nobody could argue with Warne's record of three promotions in five seasons – they could push on and solidify their play-off hopes, perhaps even have a chance at going up automatically, but to do that the gap to the top two could not get any wider than the 12 points it already was at that early stage of the season.

'The manager came in and assessed the group and slowly we started to get to grips with the way that Paul wanted us to do things,' said Davies. 'The manager also realised our strengths and qualities which he didn't have before.'

Warne's style of play soon took hold and after a 1-0 defeat at Ipswich Town on 21 October, the next time Derby tasted a league loss would not be until 11 February when they fell 3-2 at Wycombe Wanderers. The run of 15 league games unbeaten lifted Derby from tenth all the way up to fourth and with a genuine belief they could close the gap on the top two. It was during this run that David McGoldrick drove Derby forward by hitting 11 goals – including three hat-tricks – and registering an assist. On top of that, midfielder Conor Hourihane, who started for Aston Villa against Derby in the 2019 play-off final, notched four assists and three goals to provide a true creative hub in the centre of midfield, which had arguably been missing since the Frank Lampard days.

'I think that run was right around the time when we really started to click with Paul's style of play and match it up with our personnel,' Davies said. 'We would switch to a back four more often to help match the type of players that we had and I think that helped us during that run.'

The run had Derby rapidly climbing the table and not only did they believe they could cement their play-off credentials, there was a genuine feeling they could go up automatically.

'I think that's part of what started our poor form,' Davies said. 'We were on a solid run, and the top three weren't in great form themselves. There was a point when we played Plymouth away [on 7 March 2023], and we started eight points behind them but with a chance to go five behind them and into third position. And during that game we went from 1-0 up, to drawing, to then losing – I thought the late penalty was dubious. So in one game you've got such a big points swing, and the emotional side of it as well. I think mentally we adjusted to thinking we need to be in the top six here. But I think then we were looking behind us rather than ahead of us in the table. I think we had a bit of a mentality shift there.

'You can say its tiredness, or that we didn't maybe freshen the squad up in January, but I think when you look at some of the games they were crazy how we didn't win them. Portsmouth at home in the penultimate game of the season, we were dominant. We should have been out of sight before they scored. The MK Dons draw [1-1 at home on 10 April] was ridiculous. We had over 20 shots and about 60 per cent of the ball, they had two on target I think. But they scored from one. And we waste chances. So that is not through tiredness for me – I think it was something else. And obviously Derby are a big team for a lot of these teams in League One. We're a scalp for them so we'd often get teams right at it.'

The low moments were beginning to become more frequent on the pitch as it looked as though the long season was finally beginning to take its toll on the Rams, but throughout it Warne kept perspective for a club he believed could still achieve their ultimate ambition.

Davies continued, 'Paul was very philosophical about it all. He bites his tongue well after a game and watches games back too. He'll still say what he thinks but he'll always be calm and ask questions of the boys and try to understand from them about what was wrong or what we could have done better. Because sometimes we lose a game but we thought we played well. But good or bad, he always saves proper judgement for the Monday when you're in the analysis room. Then he'll have clipped up everything so he can have an unemotional way of looking at things.'

The rocky final third of the season, in which Derby only won seven of their final 19 matches from the end of January, meant that their play-off hopes rested on the final day in a tantalising clash against Darren Moore's Sheffield Wednesday. Derby's fall had been unforeseen after such a long run of success but they were still sixth, and would have confirmed their post-season place the previous week had they managed to beat Portsmouth at Pride Park.

The Owls had already confirmed their spot in the play-offs and were guaranteed to finish in third place in the League One table. But all notion that they would heavily rotate and take the game lightly were thrown away with Moore's pre-match press conference comments:

'We will approach the game exactly the same as others. Same precision, same details, same understanding, same commitment as the previous 45 games. As far as we're concerned we carry on as normal.

'We know how the game will be deemed for them [Derby] in terms of the severity of the match. But there is a severity for both clubs really in terms of the competitive nature of the match. It's a good game. We've equalled a club record of 93 points, so anything better means we've set a new record – so there's that from our aspect and being at home in front of our crowd. That is significant for us in terms of keeping that positivity going.'

After the disappointment of missing out on automatic promotion – Plymouth and Ipswich taking the top two spots with 101 and 98 points respectively – Moore very much saw the final game against a strong Derby side as a 'season starts now' moment. The Owls had endured their own frustrations and a dip in form from mid-March where they went winless in six, dropping points to the likes of Forest Green Rovers (losing 1-0 to the side that eventually finished bottom), Cheltenham Town and Oxford United (drawing against both). They bounced back with a confident 3-0 victory over Accrington Stanley on 10 April, which once again put them at the top of the table. But it was followed up by a bitter 3-2 defeat against bottom-half Burton Albion five days later before they got back to winning ways beating Bristol Rovers, Exeter City and Shrewsbury Town heading into their clash with Derby. But for Moore's men, the dropped points against Burton were enough for Ipswich to leap into second place in League One and never relinquish the spot.

Wednesday hosted their end-of-season awards after the 3-0 victory over Shrewsbury and what Moore saw was incredibly encouraging:

'What I liked about Sunday evening [1 May, the night of the dinner] was that the players were able to engage with the supporters. And that was the most important thing. That togetherness and we're all as one. That was implemented over the game at Shrewsbury and on the evening of the awards. And that was a pivotal moment between players and supporters.'

Derby needed to at least match seventh-placed Peterborough United's result at fourth-placed Barnsley to secure their spot in the play-offs and not leave anything to chance. A win would guarantee their place, and even though promotion would have been a 'bonus', as David Clowes put it during his BBC Radio Derby interview in July 2023 to mark a year since his takeover, the fact that the club had a chance to return to the Championship at the first time of asking was a big incentive – but there were no feelings of pressure.

'The lads have put us in a good position and we just go into the game pretty fearless and just try and play our best,' Warne told RamsTV in the build-up to the game. 'It isn't easy [Peterborough's visit to Barnsley] if truth be told. I'm well aware that during the game if I see the Derby end go up and the ball is out of play then Barnsley might have scored. But it's not really in our nature to get a draw. We're going to try and win from the outset so I'd rather defend by having the ball in their half.'

There was also a scenario whereby Derby, had they secured a top-six finish, would have played Wednesday again but there was to be no overthinking from Warne heading into game one of a potential three-match tussle.

'It's not about not wanting to show Darren my hand,' Warne told RamsTV. 'I'm really friendly with Darren anyway so he'll virtually guarantee how I'm going to play and what I'm going to do. So it's not about not showing my hand. It's just about getting through. There's no point in being coy and not getting to the play-offs but being able to say, "You won't believe what I'd have done in the next game." So we'll go as strong as we can and play as well as we can.'

The match had a smattering of chances in the first half, with Derby looking the more likely. David McGoldrick tested Cameron Dawson from 20 yards and he and Nathaniel Mendez-Laing linked up to force a piece of shaky Owls defending to keep the score at 0-0. But the afternoon flipped a series of moments which would be brutal, controversial and ultimately heartbreaking.

An under-hit back pass from Davies to Joe Wildsmith, with Callum Paterson closing in, meant the goalkeeper was stretching to clear and he could only tap the ball into the path of Marvin Johnson. Davies then cut across Johnson in an attempt to make the challenge but the Wednesday man took a tumble inside the box, and Davies was sent off for the resulting foul. Wednesday's Michael Smith scored from the penalty spot, and with Peterborough already 1-0 up at Barnsley and on their way to a 2-0 victory, Derby's promotion dreams were heading for a painful end.

'I went into the changing room and for the first two minutes my world was just circling around me. It was bizarre. But then straight away I got dragged away for a drugs test,' Davies revealed. 'I'm trying to calm my emotions just in case the lads come in – I didn't want them to see me crying, I wanted to gee them up. But then I got taken away for a drugs test. That was interesting. It gave me a different focus so I wasn't actually thinking about what had happened.

'The philosophical way of looking at things was that the play-off chances were not ruined by that singular action – it was a 46-game season. We had enough opportunities throughout the season to get into the play-off position. However, my professional integrity says, "I've let the team down." I didn't believe it was a penalty, I've had people within the game tell me it wasn't a penalty. It doesn't mean anything to me because ultimately I was sent off, and if I don't play the back pass slightly short, it doesn't happen. So I take accountability.

'It is too easy to blame the referee. I do believe he was wrong, and I don't believe it was a sending off, but at the same time I understand I gave the referee the opportunity to make that decision. And that's the thing I am most sorry for Derby fans, and for myself as well.

'I appealed the decision. It wasn't going to get us to the play-offs, it wasn't going to do anything to fix the damage. But I felt so strongly it was the wrong decision. One of the first lines of the appeal was the panel didn't believe there was enough contact for it to be a penalty, and if there isn't enough contact for a penalty then it can never be a red card. However, once the referee has decided it was a penalty, it has to be a red card. It made no sense to me.

'In VAR – and I know it's not the same because we're talking after the fact here – but in VAR if they deem the incident not to be a red card, they rescind it and the player goes back on the pitch. For me, I think if that was game 24 of the season, with not as much riding on it, I think my red card would have been rescinded. I lost the appeal, and I think I lost it partly because of how bad the optics would've looked had they rescinded it because of everything on the line in that game.'

The resulting penalty would be the only goal of the game as Derby's season came to a devastating halt. A play-off place, which was in their own hands right until the final day, had slipped through their fingers. Emotions were understandably riding high.

'Obviously we're disappointed. We haven't not got in the play-offs because of [the defeat at Hillsborough] – we had many opportunities throughout the season,' Warne told Sky Sports after the game. 'We were the better team with ten men. I can't be any prouder of the group. We just needed something to go our way but it just wasn't to be.

'The lads are in tears in there as you would expect. This is 11 months' work and it all comes down to one clearance off the line [Max Bird's second-half effort being cleared in front of goal was the closest the Rams went to an equaliser] and you're not in the play-offs.'

Davies was one of those in tears in the dressing room. The centre-back collected his thoughts over the next few days before delivering a statement to Twitter on 8 May.

'Heartbroken! For the club that I love... For all the fans that made it my home from the moment I came here... For my team mates, the management team and all the staff... And lastly for myself,' he wrote. 'I know the playoffs were decided over a 46 game season and it isn't all about this moment however. I'm gutted that I couldn't help us over the line but also devastated that this potentially will be my last action in a Derby shirt.

'No formal decision has been made regarding my future just yet and I will update you all with any news when I have it. Just know that every time I put on that shirt it was always a proud moment for me and I gave absolutely everything.

'This club is part of me now and that will never change.'

Though Davies left a window of hope that he would be back in a Derby shirt for the 2023/24 season, he knew that almost certainly he wouldn't be. And on 10 May that proved to be the case when he was officially released.

'Even though I played the last few games, I was prepared to be released,' Davies said. 'I knew the manager was going to want to get his own players in, and I saw it as there was no wrong answer – if I stayed or if they felt it was time to move on.

'If anything I think it would have been trickier for me had Derby offered me something, but told me that I wouldn't have played every game and I'd have to be a rotation player. I think that would've been tougher for my integrity. I didn't want to be a squad player.

'The fact that the decision was made for me, it made me more relaxed. My summer was a lot cleaner and a lot more relaxed because I didn't have to worry about my game time, or how the manager sees me in his plans for the next season.'

Of course it was not the end for just Davies. James Chester and Richard Stearman were also let go, signifying a huge shuffling of the pack in defence. David McGoldrick also left after 25 goals and seven assists in all competitions to go back to his first club, Notts County, on a two-year deal. Krystian Bielik was sold to Birmingham and Jason Knight left for pastures new, signing for Bristol City for a reported £2m move. But the mass outgoings did not mean the Rams were in strife.

Very few of the team who had suffered the bruising over the last few seasons remained. Only Max Bird, Louie Sibley, Craig Forsyth, Eiran Cashin and Liam Thompson were left standing from the squad which stared liquidation in the face.

Warne's recruitment drive had all the hallmarks of his style of play being implemented during his first full season in charge. Left-back Callum Elder and right-sided player Joe Ward were brought in from Hull City and Peterborough respectively to give the team more natural wing-backs. Warne called on a familiar face in former Rotherham striker Conor Washington, as somebody who would press from the front in the manner the manager wanted. Centre-backs Sonny Bradley and Curtis Nelson were brought in from Luton Town and Blackpool respectively to restock the centre-back cupboard.

David Clowes told BBC Radio Derby that he felt the budget Warne had been given for the 2023/24 season was enough to improve the squad substantially:

'Paul has been given a budget, I think a good budget for League One that is good enough to get us out of the league. But it's football and nothing is guaranteed.'

That last sentence is more true than ever – a sign that Clowes fully knew the belly of the beast, and also that Derby had experienced several lifetimes of football in just four seasons. In 2019 they were fingertips away from being a Premier League side, but football is a cruel game. Instead their road went down a much more tumultuous path which resulted in them being days away from extinction. Their fall was mighty, but pride had once again been restored.

The road back to the riches of the Premier League has never seemed so far away, but the building process has perhaps never been so straightforward for the club. A roadmap to success has begun under the stewardship of David Clowes. The obstacles will be plenty, but Derby County are no longer handcuffed to a misery which threatened to drain the club of all life. There is once again Pride at Pride Park.